TINY

KING OF THE ROADSIDE VENDORS

Sharon Graves Hall

CLOUDCAP

Cover Art and Inside Illustrations by Jim Hays
Design and Typesetting by Gary Shinn Design
Edited by Bill Bates

Published in North America by:
CLOUDCAP, P.O. Box 761, Snohomish, WA 98291-0761

ISBN 0-938567-29-2

Manufactured in the United States of America

DEDICATION

To Mrs. Ardella Gerry, my high school English teacher for sharing her love of language and literature.

SPECIAL THANKS
FOR THE SUPPORT OF FAMILY AND FRIENDS:

Bill Hall, Jennifer Hall, Virginia and Gary Graves,
Dean Slechta, Dorothy and Joe Clayton,
Barbara and Bill Bates, Diana Robinson,
Susan Cedergreen, Pete Matson,
Nola and Harold Hensley,
Marsha and Scott Green, Bill Tarver,
Ron Doane, Ken Doane, Ron Bromfield,
Mike Edwards, Frances Key, Noreen Becker,
Dorothy Spanjer, Bob Spanjer, and Judy Sells.

CONTENTS

PREFACE

In the early years after World War II, the small town of Cashmere, home of Aplets and Cotlets, nestled in the rain shadow of the Cascade Mountains in Washington State, went about its daily business. Lives centered around the industry of the community, the growing and marketing of fruit. This was orchard country where the Apple was King. The people thrived. Year after year.

Changes came, but as much as things changed they remained the same. The cycle of life was enacted many times over. Birth. Life. Death. Each life a story. Lives touched lives forming the memory trail of a lifetime.

One such life was about to explode onto the scene, reach into the outside world, and bring it home in a unique way. It would burst into a life song that would celebrate in chords both harmonic and discordant the spirit of one human being. Like a musical composition: andante, allegro, crescendo, finale, this story would begin gradually, increase in intensity, play briskly and lively, and then end abruptly.

Fate would dictate only a brief visit.

For that moment in the life of Cashmere, the face of the familiar would change. It would be a "Tiny" change.

—Sharon Graves Hall

FOREWORD

I knew Tiny for several years before I met him. By his signs. They were everywhere: nailed to trees, fence posts, barn walls and telephone poles, from Washington State to eastern Montana, the Canadian border to northern California. Counting signs was our favorite ploy for keeping children occupied on long road trips and, as a favorite in the sign sweepstakes, *"Tiny's, Cashmere, Wash."* gave us more quiet mileage than all the other well-known entries of the day, such as The Stinker of Idaho, Wall Drug of South Dakota and Burma Shave.

Unable to contain our curiosity, we rolled into Cashmere one hot summer day and stopped at Tiny's, a fruit stand which, if measured end to end, might have overlapped the goal posts of a standard football field. Our brood piled out to romp in the parking lot while Barbara and I surveyed the eye-popping displays of red and yellow Delicious apples and ripe Hale peaches, trying to decide how much we could afford on a tight budget. As we thought about it, we became conscious of a presence, perhaps a shadow blotting out the sun.

We turned around. There was Tiny! And **there** was Tiny. I'm six-foot two-inches (or was then) and this cheerful giant towered above me, Gulliver to a couple of Lilliputians. Hands on hips, he impressed me as a mixture of the Colossus of Rhodes and the Jolly Green Giant.

"Hi, folks," he greeted us. "Finding what you want? Peaches, apples, maybe a jug of cold cider?"

We wondered if the peaches were ripe.

"Ripe?" he said. "We don't sell anything else!" Then, while we gaped in astonishment, he grabbed a peach out of the case, thrust it into his mouth, bit down and consumed a good half of it on the spot, disregarding the juice which trickled from the corners of his mouth. Then he handed us each a peach and we bit into our samples with equal relish, albeit somewhat more delicately. Three people sharing a moment of pure animal pleasure.

It wasn't until I met Sharon Hall years later that I learned there was much more to Tiny Graves than the picture we carried away that afternoon.

Starting with his sheer size and legendary physical strength, one had only to scratch the surface, it seems, to find a complete human being, brimming with kindness and tenderness one moment, single-minded ambition the next—driving himself and others toward impossible goals, on occasion giving way to uncontrollable rages. He took financial risks that would have given pause to a Wall Street junk bond dealer, built, on a mountain of debt, what surely must have been the biggest fruit stand in the nation at that time, and was well on his way to becoming a roadside tycoon when his candle, burning brightly at both ends, without warning guttered and went out.

I am one of thousands who knew the surface Tiny. In the sensitive portrayal which follows, his kid sister has endowed the cardboard character in my memory with flesh and blood. We start with a sketch of the community in which he was raised, the kind Thornton Wilder must have had in mind when he wrote *Our Town*. After we pick up some fragmentary childhood memories, we come to grips with a short-lived entrepreneurial career that shot up like a sky rocket, exploded and expired in a shower of sparks. This book is about a "one-of-a-kind." There will never be another Tiny Graves. If you didn't know him then, this book may be as close as you ever get to him.

—BILL BATES, *former publisher, Snohomish County Tribune*

1

A NICE PLACE FOR A PILLOW

*Robert Frost wrote
"Home is the place where when you have to go there,
they have to take you in."
I add only that home is where one's pillow is;
where one can snuggle down.*

Cashmere is the place so many of us loved. Dick did, too. A sophisticated urbanite might find Cashmere just a little hokey, but to those of us who came from this small town, it makes little difference what others may think. We know it is good.

Cashmere is a part of who I am and what I've become. Cashmere is a community with a strong sense of itself. Confident. A little sassy. Proud. Independent. Its people reflect these traits. Collectively, Cashmere is content with its place and its purpose in the scheme of things. I don't imply the town is without fault. It isn't. It can be gossipy and narrow, fractious and petulant. It is, after all, made up of human beings. On the other hand, it can be warm and giving when the chips are down.

Neither is this town self-conscious. It is a "what-you-see-is-what-you-get" kind of a place. No pretense, please. Just be yourself. There is little patience in Cashmere for a phony.

Customers at Tiny's often said, "Cashmere is so pretty. It seems like a nice place to live." I agreed, believing it true on both counts. Of course, Cashmere was home and never having known anything else, I had no reason to think otherwise.

Part of what this book is about is family and its influence. Anyone from a small town knows that the extended family, the community, has a marked affect on one's sense of self. It is almost as though the community has a personality of its own. Emotional ties that extend beyond the front door cannot be ignored. One knows one's neighbors. People anticipate the nod of the head, the wave of the hand, and the smile of recognition when passing one another on Main Street, at the drugstore, the service station, the grocery store and the post office. Always there is the knowing and the being known. One does not move among strangers in a small town.

A special bonding develops from being in the same place and having shared experience over many years. Friendships through all the school years mean relationships with other parents who become "second moms" and "second dads". A sense of unity and common purpose comes from attending the same schools, worshiping in the same churches and playing at the same places. When second and third generation families continue to live in and support the community, the bonds become even tighter. Life histories of others become a part of one's own, not only for a period in life, but also from the beginning to the end — the span of life. Early acceptance, lifelong friendships, and identity that results from being a part of something comes easily in a small town.

Roots. Stability. Continuity.

We didn't have to look for our place. We were born into it. Even for those of us who have left for the "big time", connections remain —touchstones to community roots.

This is not to assume such benefits cannot be found in a big city. They can. I simply suggest that in Cashmere it came with the territory —a given. We were small enough to be a part of the whole, rather than so big as to be only part of a part. A sense of one's self, of knowing how one fit, of being part of the continuum, came naturally. It was a comfortable way to begin. The intricate weave of life created a complex, but familiar tapestry. It was good to be a part of the pattern.

I haven't seen many changes in my hometown over the years. It looks pretty much as it did in the '50's. Oh, the store fronts are different, the population has grown a little, there's a stop light on Main Street now, the old wood frame Blewett Hotel with its second story veranda is gone and Aplets and Cotlets has expanded, but much remains the same.

The Cashmere Valley Bank, the financial center with the polished brass accoutrements asserting austere dignity, remains at the intersection of tree-lined Cottage Avenue and Division Street. The Cashmere Baptist Church still looms righteously near the heart of downtown. The Sunset Highway where it crosses Mission Creek resounds with a familiar clack-clack rhythm as tires roll across its segmented concrete surface. The Cashmere Bulldogs and entourage continue to travel to state tournaments. The town's favorite colors are, as before, orange and black and the "game" is still a number one topic for orchardists who gather early each morning clutching coffee mugs in their calloused hands. Bulldogs remain big time entertainment in this small town.

A railroad still runs through the middle of it, but in Cashmere there is no "other side of the tracks" because the

3

tracks have nothing to do with class. They are rather the business lifeline of Cashmere, itself, where hungry railroad cars sidle up, whisper close, shoulder-to-shoulder with the burgeoning warehouses to be fed sweet contributions to the world's appetite.

As it has always been, the purpose, the growing and marketing of fruit, is clear. There is cameraderie in pursuing a common goal. Hard work makes it happen. Orchardists work independently and together, confident in eventual success. Some years bring more success than others, but the belief in staying with the thing keeps the faith. This is a constant.

Schools are important, too. They are no longer the ivy-covered buildings that we knew. The old high school, the grade school, and the Francis Willard building with its tubular fire exits, those slick appendages of escape, have long since been destroyed. In their place, however, are handsome new buildings which speak to pride in schools and belief in education. This is the same. We had it, too.

We also shared together a separate and distinct place on the planet. Like a giant patchwork quilt, its green fringed edges touching the hills on all sides, our place covered a fertile valley bed. Each patch different in design and name formed the pattern. Years of work had gone into making these pieces of the earth productive orchards. Roads, like quilt seams weaving throughout the design, carried family names, generations of Cashmere folks. A historical map, a community in visual review. Small town. Big spaces.

In addition to shared purpose, community is also shared traditions. All towns have them. One that still evokes an especially warm feeling in me is meshed with that most wonderful of holidays, Christmas. It was fun to live it. It is fun to remember it.

School was out. Christmas vacation was beginning. But, first, there would be a sleighful of magic for the true believers, a visit from Santa. And what a visit it was! The old

4

gentleman in his red and white, black- belted, fluffy-bearded jolliness came to Cashmere, just to see us.

A sleepless night preceded his long awaited arrival. Before bedtime we'd gotten precise directions from moms and dads where we were to meet them after the big party next day: in front of the bakery, Blonden's Hardware, or Shafran's Department Store. These were pretty important logistics since we weren't meeting Santa at school, but downtown — all of us, kids and parents, grandmas and grandpas.

Bundled up in our winter coats, stocking caps and mittens (guaranteed against loss by the string which ran down both sleeves), we were lined up two-by-two, chattering like excited squirrels, and marched from the elementary school to the center of town. There we stood massed shoulder-to-shoulder to wiggle-wait in wide-eyed wonder for Mr. Claus. Some of us cast anxious glances to see if Mom and Dad were at the pre-determined spot and continued scanning until the designated parent appeared. Secret relief.

Suspense built along with the crowd surrounding the pint-sized participants. Everything stopped for the event. This is what we did at Christmas. Everyone who could came to town.

From street view, child height, the community tree appeared like the giant of the forest, all dressed up in his come-to-town baubles. Snow, lights, color and music were all around.

According to tradition, Hy Reike, the white-haired, boom-voiced banker, led Christmas carols. Small voices rang shrilly while eyes darted back and forth, up and down, in search of that merry guest from the North Pole. Carols. Waiting. Anxiety. Then . . . the instant when sleigh bells jingled happily in cadence with the strains of "Here Comes Santa Claus." It was the magic moment. We shared it together, big kids and little kids. Moms and Dads, friends and neighbors. The whole doggone town! Before scurrying off to meet our parents, we lined up, mittened palms thrust upward to get our bag of candy. There was a whole lot of goodness there, the good stuff of community, the filling of the memory bank for a lifetime.

Work hard. Be yourself. Look out for one another. The small town lessons rubbed off on many of us. We heard them at home, too, but we also lived up to these values with the extended family.

I've often thought of how protected we were in the Cashmere Valley during our growing up years. Surrounded physically by hills and orchards, emotionally by family and friends, it was not unlike a womb which nurtures its child until it is time to be born into the world. No "preemies", we were full term. Our families and community had nurtured us, preparing us for the next growth phase.

This was our town. This was Tiny's town. Common traditions, values and purpose drew us together. Tiny grew up with this background. He knew the folks. He knew the rules. He knew to keep to the business of Cashmere, in fact capitalizing on it.

But, even before he put up his first sign, Dick Graves had something special going for him, an intangible working in his favor: the confidence and security that family and community had given him. It made a comfortable difference. Dick had been nurtured. He had, in fact, at times been tolerated! He had known the bonds and the bounds of community.

Dick loved his hometown, choosing to come back to it. In so doing he not only became an integral part of it, he eventually became a symbol for it. He was pleased with that accomplishment.

From the beginning Dick Graves kept it simple and straightforward. His signs promoted only two places. They just happened to be the two he was proud of: "TINY'S, CASHMERE, WASHINGTON".

He asked me if I could make some signs, about twelve by twenty-four inches and I said, "Well, how many, Dick?" He said, "Oh, well, I want a lot of them. Why don't you get your gang to saw the boards, coat 'em, get 'em all primed and bring 'em in and I'll screen 'em." He had 2500 signs on that big truck at one time.

I said, "What are you going to do with all those signs, Dick?" And he said, "Well, I'm going to put 'em up all around these places. Boy, they'll know where Tiny's is when I get through."

When they went down south, they'd take a bunch of signs with them and Dean would take his climbers and climb a tree, way up there . . . seventy-five feet in the air. When I asked Dick if they were going to make him take them down, he said, "If they want them down, they can take them down." We saw them in Utah on those fence posts along the railroad tracks. He put them every three quarters of a mile or so. A lot of them didn't stay up, but a lot of them did.

—PETE MATSON, sign painter and friend

2

A CHILD'S-EYE VIEW

Even though we live in the world as adults,
there remains in us a child .
. . a child who remembers another lifetime
when all experience was first-impression vivid.
Houses were bigger, hills were steeper,
storms were scarier, nights were darker,
clowns were funnier, the earth was closer and life was forever.

I t was the 'Forties. There was a war. I was brand new. I didn't know anything. Gary was two. He didn't know much either. Babies don't understand things like Pearl Harbor and blackouts and sugar rations. My big brother, Dick, did, though. He wasn't brand new. He was very old. He was ten. We had parents, too. Duke and Doris. They were nice.

As a baby I don't remember my big brother. Mom said he liked me, though. When they brought me home from the hospital, he didn't pinch me or anything. He wanted to hold me, but he was scared of me. He said, "She's so small. Look at her little fingernails." He gave me back to Mom. She said he was afraid my head would fall off or something. It didn't.

(Although scared of babies, Dick was afraid of little else. Even at the age of four, Mom told me his penchant for risk-taking asserted itself when he accepted a neighbor's challenge in the Great Mud Pie Caper which I tell about in detail later on.)

I started remembering when I was three. That was the year Gary accidentally hit me in the eye with a hoe; a dog bit me and now I have a dimple there. I had to wear corrective shoes because I was pigeon-toed; I had to have little round glasses because I was cross-eyed; my finger got cut off in a car door; and I was flower girl in Aunt Gwendolyn's wedding.

Gary was the ring bearer. I forgot to drop the petals. We got the giggles. My dress was blue. Mom gave me a permanent in one of those machines with all the wires hooked to the curlers. I didn't like it. Then I looked funny. Orphan Annie. Gary was cute. Gary was always cute.

I don't know where Dick was. He must have been at school because he wasn't home on those days when Mom made lemon meringue pie and I got to lick the beaters. He wasn't home when I played choir director either. He would have laughed. Mother didn't laugh. She said I was pretty good. The towel on my head for long hair and the *Reader's Digest* for the hymnal were O.K. with her. I could sing, too . . . "Holy, Holy, Holy", "Jesus Loves Me", and "This Little Light of Mine." I remember Dick and Gary slept in the same room. They had twin beds.

Dick wasn't much fun. He always wanted to sleep. I had my own room. My bedroom set had a dresser with a mirror and little arms that swung out. Mom put a skirt with ruffles on them.

My bed fell down sometimes and there were snakes under there! In the closet, too. Gary and I had a code. We would knock on the paper-thin wall. Dick would say "Be Quiet!" We would get the giggles. Then he would really get mad. He didn't like to play with us.

Sometimes Mom would say to Gary and me, "O.K., now let's see who can go to sleep first. Then I would tell Gary, "I'm asleep first!" Then he would say, "Huh-uh, I am."

"Huh-uh."

"Uh-huh."

"Huh-uh."

"Uh-huh."

Dick would say, "Quiet!" Guess he was asleep first.

(With two much younger siblings to boss around, Dick was already developing the habit of command that would serve him well as one of Cashmere's most enterprising employers.)

Dick laughed when my bed fell down. He fixed it for me, though. He wasn't afraid of those snakes. Dick went to school. He went on the yellow school bus and he had a lunch pail with a thermos. It had a little wire that kept his milk from rolling around. One time he broke it. Then his milk rolled around.

Dick was mostly gone. Gary and I played. One time we took a jar of marshmallow creme from the top shelf. We got two spoons. We sat on the front porch steps and ate the whole thing, but we put back the empty jar. Mom said there must have been some pretty big mice in the house. We were sure lucky about those mice.

Mostly then I remember Gary . . . and the blue jay in the pine tree outside my window. I talked to it in the mornings. He didn't talk my talk so we talked his.

And there were the mice that time, out by the cistern in the flower garden, right next to the columbine and the old spirea bush. They didn't have any eyes. They were all wiggly and pink. Their mom wasn't there, either. Poor things. Mom said she didn't like mice. Dick said he'd like to drown them. I put them in a shoe box. They died. Guess their mom didn't know where they went.

Sometimes Dick babysat for us. He went to his room. Gary locked me outside. I didn't have any shoes on.

We had a swing. Dad made it. I could swing almost as high as Gary. I knew that I could fly if I went high enough. Gary said I couldn't. I think I did. I can remember looking down like I was flying right over Cashmere. Nobody believed me.

Dick had a dog. Its name was Butch. It was buff. It ran away. It lived at the Carters. We had its brother. Its name was Buff. It was black. It lived with us. We had John, too. He was Aunt Edna's and Uncle Ray's dog. I don't know why we had him. He liked Dick and rode with him in the jeep. He snapped at us and hid behind the wood stove in the kitchen when we were around, so we would poke sticks at him and make him growl and show his teeth. Then Gary and I would run and hide. Mom said it was no wonder John didn't like us. He didn't like us first, though. He started it!

In the winter we went sledding on the big hill. We took turns watching for cars. Sometimes Dick would tie a rope to the back of the car and pull us on the sled. He wasn't supposed to. We didn't tell.

In the summer we went swimming at the Cashmere pool. We must have gone there a million days. It was the best time. The pool was right at the park by the Boy Scout building. Dick was a Scout. Gary wanted to be one, too. He was a Cub.

(Growing up with reverence for all the cherished American institutions— Scouting, home, school, patriotism, church —Dick was ill-prepared for the hippie revolution of the 1960's

We always took money when we went to the pool. Then we could go to the little market by Town's Feed Store. We never wore shoes and we burned our feet when we ran to the store. We hopped along on our tippy toes and on the sides of our feet. We stopped in the shadows. It wasn't melty and hot there.

At the store we bought Lik-maid sticks and those little wax things with the sweet liquid inside. We got pop out of the cooler with the water in it. The pop hung from the lids and we slid them along their little slots until they came to the end. Then we took them out and opened them with the opener on the side of the cooler. I liked Orange Crush in the brown bottles. But it was always hard to decide.

Dick was a big show-off when he went to the pool. He would run out to the end of the board, jump as hard as he could and make a big splash. He cracked the board one time and they wouldn't let him do that anymore.

(From show-off to showman was just a short step.)

We spent a lot of time listening to the radio. Everything began with "The": The Green Hornet. The Shadow. The Whistler. The Lone Ranger. One time Dad surprised Mom with a new Packard Bell radio. She cried. We could get programs from far away and best of all it made records. It had a microphone and two arms, one to make the records and one to make them play back.

It was fun to make the records. They were black or orange or green and when the needle made the sound the colored fuzz would come up on the top of the record where the needle had been. Gary and I thought it was magic. Guess it was. Dad and Mom had friends who would get together and play music. Then they would record it on the Packard Bell.

On Friday nights we all went to the movies. I sat with Mom and Dad. Gary sat with his friends. Dick sat in the loges. Sometimes Dick worked at the theater.

The ushers were neat. They wore uniforms with rows of little buttons and they walked up and down with their flashlights so we could see where to go. They stood at the back and let people in through the curtains.

On Saturdays Gary and I went to the movies with the kids to see the serials. I liked Superman, but we saw the Lone Ranger and Hop-along Cassidy, too. We ate popcorn and Black Crows and Milk Duds. The theater burned down. Too bad.

Mostly we didn't see Dick. He played football and we went to see him and people would yell, "Look at that Graves. Knocked a hole right out of the middle. Boy, can he tackle!" He and Bob "Bubbles" Purcell were pretty good. Everyone said so. They were very big. We yelled for both of them.

After the war was over Dad bought Mom a new car. It was a black Fleetline Chevrolet. Dad let Dick drive it. Dick drove too fast. He wrecked it.

(Dick drove like he raced through life — at top speed. He was to give Mom, highway patrolmen and others many anxious moments.)

Then Dick went to college in Cheney. He went to play football. He did that for two years. Then he went into the army. When he came home he brought us presents and we thought his army picture on the radio was pretty nice. His socks were folded neat, too. He made us do ours the same way. Guess it was the right way.

He was at the Presidio in San Francisco right by the Golden Gate Bridge. He told Gary and me that sometime he would take us there. (Later, he did.) He sent lots of pictures of it.

It was fun to go to the post office to look for the postcards. Mom taught us how to open the box. We took turns. We argued about turns. I remember how to do it. Once around to f and $1/2$, back up to g and $1/2$, and back to h. Box 102, Cashmere.

Once Dick sent us one of those great big bundles of postcards that unfold and get real long. It had pictures on both sides. It said Hollywood right on the front.

When I was at Camp Fire camp at Lake Wenatchee, he sent me a box of salt water taffy from San Francisco. It was enough for the whole cabin.

Later we got pictures of Dick in his uniform when he was an M.P. Dick was an honor guard for General MacArthur when he came to San Francisco. Mom and Dad were very proud.

Gary and I argued a lot. Sometimes we played. Mostly he wanted to play with the neighbor boys. I picked sunflowers for Mom. I don't think she liked them, though. She said they had bugs. It was fun to play by the ditch. I would sit on the edge and watch all the different things float by.

Sometimes I went to see Mrs. Charleton. She was very old. One-hundred and fifty, I think. She lived across the field. On the way to her house I would walk by the hazelnut trees to see if there were any nuts on the ground. She said it was all right to eat them. I cracked them with rocks.

We sat in her green and white striped swing and talked. She had a hammock, too. It was tied to two pine trees. It was so high I had to struggle to into it. When I did get into it, I fell out.

She had a little pool with a fountain. It was fun to play there in the summer. She would turn it on just for me. I pretended it was my own pool.

There was a big wooden cross on the hill by her house. People came there on Easter. Guess that's where Jesus died.

Some days she would dry apricots. It was fun to watch them wrinkle up in the sun.

She baby sat for Gary and me. She gave us little peppermint puff balls for a treat. They were good. Once we took some more when she wasn't looking. Her house was dark. One room she never used. She called it the parlor. Sometimes we could go look at it. There was a lamp shade in there with fringe all around the bottom. It was pink.

Dick didn't visit Mrs. Charleton very often, but he liked that old car she had in her garage. He said he would sure like to get his hands on that. She only drove it to town when she got her groceries. I liked her. She was a nice lady.

Charlie Williams and Queenie were my friends, too. Queenie was brown and white. She was a bird dog. Charlie said she wouldn't know a bird if she saw one, though. Queenie slept a lot. Charlie wore striped overalls and he always had a shovel. Said he killed a snake with it right by the big pine tree where I waited for him to come and check his waterbox. Said he hit its head with the shovel and that I should always watch out for rattlesnakes. I did.

He called me "Suzie Q". "How you doin', Susie Q?" he would say. I liked that. Charlie was Dick's friend, too. He was everybody's friend. Sometimes he and Mrs. Williams would let me come down and look at his arrowhead collection. The arrowheads were in black frames and they were all in rows. He had found some of them in the orchards.

We moved away from Flowery Divide when Dad bought a bigger orchard at Yaxon Canyon. He and Roy Dugwyler were partners. Dad built a new house and he bought us a buckskin horse. Her name was Ginger. She got out a lot. Dad said the horse was smarter than we were. I didn't think so. Gary and I played Monopoly with the Dugwylers and the

Phillips and the Harndens. We had more friends. That was nice, but I missed Mrs. Charleton and Charlie and Queenie. Things changed. I didn't pick sunflowers anymore.

(Through childhood and pre-adolescence, I remained in blissful ignorance of the mysterious influences that changed my older brother from a happy-go-lucky boy into a man possessed by ambition and driven by unknown demons toward impossible goals.)

In the very beginning, when Dick was going to do a fruit stand, I worked at DeBord Fruit Company and I knew Dick from high school. He came in one day and bought every jug of cider and every watermelon we had. So we were curious as to what he was doing with all this cider so when he came into the office one day to pay for it, I said, "Dick Graves, what are you doing with all that cider?" And he said, "I'm going to sew up every gallon jug of cider in this valley." And I wondered why. He was going to start a fruit stand. You couldn't buy cider. You couldn't buy it in the grocery stores. You couldn't buy it anywhere. The only way you could get cider was to go to Tiny's. And that was his gimmick. Cider King. He used to come in there with that big truck and they loaded that with watermelon and his first fruit stand, all that was there were watermelons and cider. I mean cider stacked as high as you could stack it. That was his gimmick.

And he would come in there and, honest to God, every gallon of cider we had went to Tiny. He had a deal set up. I don't know how he did it, but that was the only way you could get cider was through Dick and his fruit stand. I was always so interested in him because of all this stuff that was going on. —NOLA HENSLEY

(Nola Hensley, a resident of Dryden, knew Tiny from high school days and worked one summer in the fruit stand.)

3

WHEN BIG BROTHER WENT TOO FAR

Dick was somewhat of a father figure to me,
partly because he was ten years older than I
and partly because he was so protective.
On more than one occasion this became a problem
as he tried to control me through his view of the world.
One evening he went too far.

It happened at the end of a double date which included the weekly Rainbow dance at the Masonic Hall where we danced to the recorded music of Glen Miller and Johnny Mathis for the cheek-to-cheek stuff and Elvis, Chubby Checker and the Everly Brothers for the jitterbug.

The dance was followed by the second social event of the evening, the ritual gathering at George's, the local hamburger stand where everyone ordered his or her own version of the Great American Hamburger. Mine was with ketchup and pickles only, please. We kids stood around, visited from car to car or cruised our favorite circular route up through town and back down and around George's. It was American Grafitti, Cashmere style. Pretty innocent

17

stuff and, as such, the scene of my whereabouts until we decided it was time to go home.

The time then: after 1 a.m. The place: our driveway. The principal players: me, my date, my friend, her date, and my brother. As the plot unfolded, Dick gave one of his Academy Award winning performances.

As we sat in the car, talking and listening to the radio, my friends and I were stunned into silence by the abrupt and dramatic arrival of the big white "Tiny" Oldsmobile which tore into the yard, engulfing us in a thick cloud of dust and nearly sideswiping us. Dick then swung around in front of our car as if to block any attempt to exit, hurled himself from his car and, drawing his huge frame up in his most menacing pose, planted himself in front of us, hands on hips, glowering at the boys. They were totally intimidated. I was embarrassed and confused and, at the same time, angry. It all had happened so fast!

Evidently when I hadn't come home by midnight, Dick appointed himself my personal curfew officer! Anyway, with the same quickness he had materialized in front of us, he wheeled around and charged into the house, nearly taking off the door as he went. (That sturdy back door withstood the tantrums of three Graves kids over the years.) He wasn't content with upsetting us. He marched on through the house, woke up Mom and Dad and barked, "Do you know it's after one o'clock and Sharon is still out in the car?" Dad sensed that Number One son had probably done something stupid.

Would Dick please explain what this was all about? Yes. He would. He did. Ha! Now **he** was in trouble. Dad told him in no uncertain terms that he was out of line, I wasn't, and he had embarrassed me in front of my friends. If Dick wasn't careful, he was going to create some real problems.

Dad had spoken. Typically, Dick's emotional outbursts were followed by periods of contrition. He was sorry, but what now?

The timing was right. As I sat in the car sulking, trying to convince my friends that my brother wasn't going to kill them, and refusing to go in, Dick was busy creating the penitential offering.

And what delicacy did he prepare? Sliced peaches, hot tea and buttered toast. My girlfriend, who I'm sure was having misgivings about staying all night, joined me in this early morning snack as we sat down at the table where place settings for two had been carefully arranged. How could we resist?

Fortunately for our relationship, he never did anything that heavy handed again. Dad was clearly the last word, even to "Tiny, the Cider King".

One day, a salesman came in with an idea for a custom tee shirt with Tiny's logo, an apple with a worm coming out of the it. He said "I would like you to try a few of these, Tiny, and see how they sell. Tiny asked the wholesale price and I think it was forty-nine cents with a price break on six dozen.

"Send me four-hundred and I'll see how they go," Tiny said. Well, the salesman was elated to think he had sold about thirty-four dozen tee shirts. Luckily, he found out in time that Tiny was ordering four-hundred dozen. That's how he did business. —BILL TARVER

(Bill Tarver, a Cashmere insurance agent, was a long-time friend of Tiny's and often helped out in the parking lot at the fruit stand)

19

4

JUST BEFORE THE EXPLOSION

*Good times at the house on Flowery Divide,
the sunflower springs, the columbine and spirea,
the swing, the sledding hill . . . all that ended.
Life moved on. It slid right into the next decade.*

It was the 'Fifties. Happy days. Elvis Presley, "Rock Around the Clock", Bill Haley and the Comets. Cherry cokes and white bucks were the rage. Television was a novelty. The snowy pictures on our first black and white set in 1954 brought us a new view of the world through American Bandstand, Mickey Mouse Club and the Ed Sullivan Show. We were the first generation to come under the powerful influence of the new medium in our living room. TV babies.

Life still centered around the community, television notwithstanding. Those were days when, as normal kids, we gathered at the drug store after school and on Saturday mornings, consuming flavored Cokes, Green Rivers or sodas with real ice cream. Sometimes we ordered plain Cokes and emptied a five-cent bag of peanuts into them. Good.

The curved counter with the swivel chairs became our favorite childhood hang-out. At night, as we grew older (and bolder), we often could be found at George's Drive-in for hamburgers and cokes until, in our later teens, we preferred disappearing two-by-two into the canyons and orchards for more private conversations with our current love.

On weekends we followed the Cashmere Bulldogs and went to school and Rainbow dances. Occasionally we ventured out of our little valley and drove to Wenatchee, ten miles away, to cruise the Avenue and make a few circles around the XXX Root Beer barrel, eager to see and be seen. Then it was a toss-up about where to get the best hamburger. Some thought Vic's, some Dusty's. I was a Dusty fan myself. Loved that sauce!

Times were simpler then but not necessarily easier. We were the Graves family, embracing the lifestyle of the era and the values of our small town. There were six of us: Mom, Dad, Dick, Gary, me and, later, Greg Hallead, a cousin who came to live with us.

Dad was the boss, a community leader, active in Lions, the Masonic Order and other community organizations. He was a good man, the final word in our family. He was strong and proud, an example of what hard work and determination could accomplish. Starting with nothing, Dad worked for years in fruit warehouses, finally becoming a foreman at the Cashmere Fruit Exchange. Eventually he saved enough money to buy an orchard.

Dad's way was the hard way. Eventually we kids followed his example. He was the family's solid "rock" until the tragic years toward the end.

If Dad was a model for the work ethic, Mom was one for gently taking life as it comes. Mother didn't demand from life. She just thoroughly involved herself with the now

21

and the what is. Her family was everything. She lived for her husband and her children, not as the familiar cliche of television sit-coms, but simply and honestly. Life in terms of "values" or "role models" or "analysis" would have been, for Mom, ridiculous. Life was to be lived as it was dealt.

It didn't take much to make Mom happy, because she felt she had it all. She was content with bowling on Thursday, fried chicken and mashed potatoes and gravy on Sunday and a wash on the line every Monday. Chicken has never since tasted so good or clothes smelled so sweet.

Eight years older than Gary and ten years older than I, Dick was in some respects almost like another father. Because of the age difference, our brother lived in different worlds: high school, college, and the Army. We loved him, but we didn't know him very well then. The experience that would bond us ever so closely was yet to happen.

In the meantime, Gary and I were just a couple of kids growing up in a small town, playing with the neighbor kids, swimming at the city pool, driving the jeep in the orchard and, through it all, arguing. Always arguing.

We were lucky, the three of us. We had good parents, a healthy family life and the freedom to be ourselves. We just grew. Life was uncomplicated, natural and easy.

I remember discipline, but I don't remember criticism. We were never made to feel we couldn't do what we set out to do. Maybe that made the difference, knowing we were loved, that we had to behave and that we were accepted as we were. Acceptance built confidence, probably the finest gift our parents gave us because life demands a lot of it. Confidence gave us "Tiny's". Dick Graves never thought he couldn't.

Our childhood was a peaceful time and our home town a nurturing place. From this background the big man from Cashmere, Washington, emerged to become a part of Northwest lore. The Korean Conflict had just ended. Dick Graves was home from the service and an explosion was in the making. It would take the form of one of the most successful small businesses our state has known.

The explosion and its lingering shock wave would also change, dramatically, the life of the Graves family. Duke and Doris's oldest son would soon create his own version of the American Dream. Why not? He was never given any reason to believe he couldn't succeed. His family loved him. His mother and father believed in him. He was back in Cashmere, a safe haven.

Dick was home and he wanted to stay. Furthermore, he knew what he wanted:

"Just a little fruit stand, Dad. Will you help me get started?" Of course Dad would. It was his son's turn to try.

The first small stand, eventually to balloon into a roadside circus, began in 1953 with few pretensions. It was known as the Buckhorn Fruitstand and stood across the street from its more important parent, the Buckhorn Cafe, a spot where orchardists gathered to sip coffee, or get a quick breakfast or lunch. Both businesses were on the Sunset Highway just inside the city limits. Every small town has such a place.

In those days, it was the "Buckhorn". Dad rented that first stand for Dick from Cecil Carter, the owner of the cafe and fruit stand.

"We'll just rent to begin with. Try it out for a summer. See if this is really what you want to do," Dad said.

Small beginnings. Big plans. We certainly had no idea then that Dick Graves and his dream would propel us onto a carousel of work, play and privilege that would change our lives. One day there was no Tiny's. The next day, there it was! I don't know how it happened. It just did. Like a dynamite charge with a slow burning fuse, the little road-side stand started innocently, smouldered slowly and then, suddenly, BOOM! It exploded.

Dick (Tiny) proclaimed himself the Cider King. His slogan, "Fruit Fit For a King", was the first of many catch phrases and sales gimmicks that would become part of his legend. Creative, seething with ambition and boiling with energy, Dick Graves specialized in the unpredictable and fresh ideas floated from his fertile brain in a steady stream.

He created his own kingdom and ruled with a determination that was fired by his vision. His creation became its own power source, feeding his imagination, driving him to keep ahead of the thing that was developing from within while manifesting itself on the outside.

How did he do it? Simple really, if one is a visionary, a risk taker and a dreamer. Dick couldn't not do it. Success was in him. His own unique view of what could be became his driving force. He didn't start out to become a legend. He simply did what he had to do and the legend followed.

Although he hadn't studied economics, Dick had an instinct for advertising, mass display and salesmanship. He was a natural. A master showman, he started by deciding, with exquisite judgement, to be himself, replete with bright, floral shirts clashing with plaid bermuda shorts, and a crown (literally).

Free to be himself, supremely self-confident, Dick ignored the normal constraints of prudence and caution.

Result: *Tiny's, Cashmere, Washington.*

I marveled at what he did (in the business). I often wished I could have done what he did. I envied him. You know a young person like that and what a terrific success. He wasn't doing it just for himself. He was doing it for the community and the kids at the school and his kids at the stand. Dick didn't have a family of his own and yet he had a bigger family than any of us. It was great to have known him.
—RON DOANE, Owner, Valley Pharmacy in Cashmere

5

ALWAYS THE UNEXPECTED

*A natural showman is born knowing
the ingredients of success:
excitement, scale, flamboyance and the unexpected.
Of these, doing the unexpected may
be the most important.*

At the time that my big brother was beginning to call attention to himself and his little fruit stand, I was in the throes of adolescence. Dick managed to capture my attention in spite of that fact, no small task since that period in one's life is centered in me, me, me. I alternated between two conflicting identities: that of Sharon Graves and Tiny's little sister.

Tiny was beginning to blossom as a showman. He got my attention, and that of others by always doing the unexpected. Seldom satisfied to let things be, he made life one continual surprise party.

Dick early developed a passion for big cars. In 1954 he bought a new Oldsmobile '98, a beautiful machine just two steps below the Number One General Motors car, the Cadillac.

What he did next I could hardly believe. He took his brand new car, one that I could vicariously enjoy, and painted the darn thing white with big red apples and the "Tiny" logo. I thought he was nuts. So did other people.

"What's that Graves kid doing anyway?"

"Did you see what he did this week? Painted that new car."

"Yeah, and did you see where Graves bought a big new Ford cabover?"

"He painted that, too."

"Where does he get the money for that kind of thing?"

"And have you seen the way he parades around in those Bermuda shorts with that crown on his head?"

"He had Highway 2 blocked on Apple Blossom weekend. There were cars and busses everywhere. We could hardly get through."

"I think he's making money over there."

"Well, he's not going to keep it if he doesn't stop spending it."

"He's put those signs up all the way to Seattle and Spokane."

"Who does he think he is?"

He thought he was Tiny, the Cider King, that's who. I don't think anyone was more intrigued with what was happening than the new monarch, himself. One thing led to another and at no point did he lack for imagination. The more he did, the more he realized what he could do.

He was having a ball.

The locals were right about the traffic jams. They were not exaggerating. The signs (by now hundreds were in place and eventually there would be thousands all over the Northwest) were leading people to Tiny's and Tiny was making sure the stop would be memorable.

I remember one of the early Apple Blossom weekends. Dick had purchased five-thousand gallons of cider and displayed most of them in four-tiered display racks outside the little stand. The display stretched for 60 feet . . . a cider extravaganza!

In Dick's mind, what may have been the world's largest cider display wasn't enough. He added snow!

Snow? Yes, snow. He used his new truck to haul all that cider to the stand, then sent his younger brother, Gary, to Stevens Pass to get truckloads of snow. Back and forth. Back and forth. All night Gary shoveled, transported and unshoveled snow.

Now ice cold and blanketed in white, the broad phalanx of cider jugs was irresistible to passing motorists.

"He was a genius. I had fogotten how beautiful and big that place was. The flowers, the music, the homemade pies. We went there every Sunday for hamburgers. I loved the way he ran that — the way I'd like to see things run. You had somebody directing you at all times. The boys were always so polite and neat."
—DOROTHY SPANJER, family friend, Cashmere

6

AN IRRESISTIBLE FORCE

*They said Tiny didn't have the chance
of a snowball in hell.
They were wrong. Some snowball!
Tiny's just kept rolling along,
gathering speed, mass and momentum.*

What does one do to keep the momentum going? If you're Tiny, you order three-thousand cans of Planter's Peanuts, display them outside your business, then go one step farther by spelling your name in red Spanish peanut cans in a field of blue blanched peanut cans. You invite "Mr. Peanut" of Planter's fame to dance a welcome to your customers and, presto! You have another happening.

Clever! Persons missing the cider in the snow on Apple Blossom weekend experienced Tiny's latest—peanuts! And, of course, salted peanuts made you thirsty and thirst required quenching. Well what do you know? Tiny solved that problem, too. Forget that he helped create it.

Tiny had them talking all the way to Seattle and Spokane and Vancouver, B.C. He was beginning to understand that he could sell anything he put his mind to . . . and his mind didn't work like anyone else's. It was different. It was the difference that created the darndest side show Highway 2 had ever known.

What next? Well, catch them coming and going. If one stand is good, two is better. If two is better then three must be best. Before long, Dick had three stands in simultaneous operation, two in Cashmere and one at the junction of Highway 2 and Blewett Pass Highway. His reasoning: if someone is going to take the time to stop at a stand, he, Tiny, was going to do all he could to make certain that stop was at one of his fruit stands. The big guy had a competitive spirit. The spoils to the winner!

With his second stand, he added food service, giving folks even more reason to stop at Tiny's.

"We'll pick up some cider and have a bite to eat." Good plan. However, one got more than a "bite to eat". One got a mouthful.

From the first slap of hamburger to grill, the intent was to build the best, and biggest, hamburger in the West. Sesame seed buns, special sauce, double meat . . . sounds familiar, doesn't it? Even before the "Big Mac" made its debut, Tiny's burgers were making a name for themselves. They were huge. They were good. They had a loyal following.

Dick wanted to sell a burger big enough to satisfy his appetite. Achieving this, it was then guaranteed to satisfy anyone else's. He was right. Many happy tummies returned again and again.

"Gotta have a Tiny Burger with fries." Dick Graves knew what he wanted and went after it. Living with his roadside sideshow became a rapid-fire, tumultuous existence. I don't recall any of us thinking at the outset that this novelty would become anything more than it was . . . an annoyance, a temporary, albeit all-consuming preoccupation with the largest member of our family. Before long, though, we were all involved in one way or another in making the little business hum in tune with Tiny's orchestration.

We hauled cider, spread sawdust, unpacked merchandise, cleaned and scrubbed, built shelves and sold merchandise. All of these menial functions needed continually to be done. Done now and done right! Tiny had a plan. Always a plan. Always a vision.

How it would all get done was generally not part of the plan. But, no problem, when one is a master persuader and has a family close at hand. Family is an easy touch. Particularly when it's "just this one time". Particularly when the family catches the spirit of the adventure and begins to share the vision.

Dreams are catching and the biggest dreamer of them all didn't hesitate to spread the germs of enthusiasm. He knew instinctively what many top executives take years to learn. Involve others. Let them experience success. Give them a sense of ownership.

Employees who are satisfied work for more than the paycheck. They work for the company. And that is exactly what his family members did in those early years. We worked for the company because there was no paycheck. The money just wasn't there. Not yet. Neither were days off. Not yet.

Dick rewarded us in other ways: dinner out, money for the weekend, and a car when we needed one.

It was OK. Gary and I learned how to work. We learned the rewards of work are more than monetary. And we learned that hard work pays off. It has made a difference. We don't think in terms of overtime. We think in terms of what is needed to get the job done.

Later Dick had the financial means to help us in many other ways. Cars, clothes, and college were among them.

He was a generous man, a good big brother. He never forgot the early years. We never have either. In some ways they were the best, the least complicated, the closest to our mutual beginnings. They were the nicest because then it was just us. The stand hadn't become the focus, the maelstrom that would suck everything into its swirling vortex.

But the fact is, Tiny's did become the focal point of our lives. It came to be a source of pride for all of us, but it was not without its price. A life that had always centered around the family eventually centered around this new creation. There would be no more family vacations at the new resort on Whidbey Island or fishing trips to Kamloops, B.C., or weeks at Green's Resort on Lake Chelan.

Oh, we would have a cabin and a boat at the lake, but we were seldom there together.

We were dealing with a new creation which would bring new fortune, both good and bad. It would affect each family member in ways that none of us could have predicted. It would bring monetary advantages never before dreamed. It would test the foundations of our roots.

Each of us would have to struggle to cope with this kinetic phenomenon which would demand so much. As beautiful as it was to become, it would rob us of an easiness, a facet of family life that would never exist again. We would become too busy with the Tiny overlay on our lives, carried along by the current of energy needed for the new "baby".

The new member of the family needed constant care. As the fruitstand grew, the time needed to nurture it became all-consuming. Its needs came first, often at the sacrifice of our personal needs. The stand was successful and we loved it, but we paid a price.

Behind the scenes the activity was frenetic, the work never ending. Dick's ideas knew no bounds. An engineer on a runaway train eating up track as fast as it could be laid down, he was not to be stopped.

Tiny's kingdom became more than a fruit stand. It

became an "event" that was hard to pass up. Tiny's blue and white signs dotted the landscape along major highways in the Northwest and beyond. White cars and trucks were adorned with big red apples and the Tiny logo. Hundreds of yellow and pink boxes of Aplets and Cotlets, thousand of gallons of amber colored cider, and nature-painted cherries, apples, plums, apricots, and peaches became a part of this new business. Add hamburgers, souvenirs, and Tiny, himself, and Tiny's became a "must stop".

We were along for the ride. Along the way we came to understand the expression, "There is no such thing as a free ride". We earned the price of our ticket and realized the payment had very little to do with money. It had to do with life, important lessons that were like a ride through Axiom Valley: "Make do", "Nothing is without its price", "Anything worth doing is worth doing well", "You never know until you try", "No one said it would be easy". We learned these and others as we scurried to keep pace with the Big Engineer.

Early on it seemed Tiny's train would roll on forever. To imagine a caboose was to think the unthinkable. Tiny was on an endless track, one that would never reach the vanishing point. What could possibly stop him?

He was an amazing salesman. He ordered a hundred dozen straw hats in all sizes and shapes and sold them in two months — in a fruit stand!
—BILL TARVER

7

MAY I HELP YOU? I WISH I COULD!

"If at first you don't succeed . . ."
Many of the days and weeks of working
at Tiny's over the years run together
but my first day on the job
is as vivid to me now as it was then.
Now I can look back and laugh,
but I wasn't laughing then and neither was Dick.
My career at Tiny's was almost finished before it began

I was 13 and ready for my first day behind the counter. As my first customers approached, I nervously reviewed in my mind how to greet them, how to make change, and generally how to behave. I knew Dick was watching. That made me nervous. I wanted to be good at this. "OK, here goes," I thought to myself.

"Hi! May I help you?"
"Yes. We'd like an ice cold glass of cider."

Good, I thought, I can handle this.
In the early 1950's we didn't yet have the cold drink dispensing machines. In order to serve a cold glass of cider

we had to open a jug from the walk-in cooler.

Into the cooler I went to retrieve the jug of juice. Because the cider bottles were vacuum sealed, we had to pry them open. Generally we used a quarter. I had seen Dick do this dozens of times. No big deal. I could handle it. Surprise! Just as I broke the seal on the jug of cider the juice spewed up and out like an eruption of Old Faithful.

I was thunderstruck. Paralyzed with disbelief. Cider was everywhere, on the displays, on the cash register, on the rafters, on me and, horror of horrors, on the customers! It was an episode out of "I Love Lucy". Towels helped clean up the mess and the customers, but my job, shaky from the start, now hung by a thread.

By then I was so shaken I couldn't concentrate on making change and ended up giving back an extra dollar. So much for profits, return customers, and possible future employment.

Fortunately, Dick was in a forgiving mood. He knew what sometimes happened if a jug had a broken seal and the juice had fermented. Not to worry. The day was young. It got old fast. It was as though Lucy had written the script.

For a reason I can't recall, Dick began hammering on a rafter on which he had perched a radio, tuned, of course, to a country western station. "Sharon," he said, "Let me know if that radio looks like it's going to fall." Easy enough. I had eyes. I had a mouth. The problem was my eyes and mouth didn't work together. What did happen, simultaneously, was my announcement that the radio was falling just as it shattered on the ground.

Unemployment loomed large.

A reprieve. Did I think I could shine the red Delicious apples and place them in the display case? I thought I could. Apples don't explode or fall from high places. I was desperate. This I had to do well. I polished those apples until they looked like glass. They were beautiful. I spent a considerable amount of time polishing apples and admiring my work. Mistake Number Three. Admiration wasn't the order of the day. When Dick returned from town, his first question was, "What have you been doing since I've been gone?"

"Shining these apples."

"Sharon, at this rate those apples will rot before you get through the whole box!"

I was crushed. The end was near.

He took me home saying we would try again the next day. Mother told me Dick had said he didn't think I was going to work out. I can't imagine why.

Fortunately for me, the next day and the day after that were better and my position at Tiny's became less tenuous and more permanent. Thank goodness Dick had a sense of humor. That we were family helped.

I can remember one time when Dick got mad. He would just swing those arms, you know, and I could seem him coming right through that fruit stand right to the kitchen door and I was the first one he saw. I had my spatula in my hand. And he started on me and finally I put that spatula up and I said, "Dick Graves, don't you ever talk to me like that again. Ever!"

He looked down at me. I hit him about the armpit. He looked kind of startled, then he howled, just started laughing his head off. "You're the funniest damn woman I ever met in my life," he said. And I went over to him and I said, "This isn't funny, Dick. I'm serious. If I've got it coming, you can tell me, but don't you ever yell at me again." From then on he never did. Everybody bowed down to him. I wasn't going to bow down to him. I mean, he was my friend. I thought the world of Dick Graves. He was always wonderful to me.

—NOLA HENSLEY

8

THE TWANG OF SUCCESS

The music was country. The beat was his own.
As family, we were gathered in and carried along.
There I was, along for a ride
that was a portent of things to come
and of things that already were.

Rhythmic, twanging country music on tour was the magnet. A white, apple-painted car caravan — country fans in response — was the result.

It was the 1950's. Tiny's Fruit Stand was an infant but some things were already clear. Tiny liked country music. Tiny liked country singers. Tiny wouldn't miss a show. Neither would we.

Family, friends and neighbors were scooped up and transported, Tiny style, to the Spokane Coliseum where we were entertained by Marty Robbins, one of country music's greats. It was the first of many occasions over the years that would put me in front row center, next to one of the biggest country fans of them all.

There is no question in my mind that those moments were the ones that brought Dick "Tiny" Graves the greatest joy and peace in his life. The words, the music, the beat, the singers, all took the big man away from the worry of his everyday life. Anyone watching him during one of the shows would have seen a vulnerable giant. Shy smile, cheeks slightly flushed, and tears revealed perhaps more than anything the sentimental man behind the signs and the legend. Country music has heart and it filled his.

In those years, Spokane, Washington, billed as the "Heart of the Inland Empire", was a mecca for those of us who lived east of the Cascades. So it was an excited little girl who looked forward to a trip to Spokane. Looking back, I conjure up images of sagebrush, the monotony of endless miles and miles of it and, finally, a sense of relief with the appearance in the distance of a pine forest, a signal that desert was behind us and we were within minutes of the Spokane highlands.

I remember vividly the sensation of coming off the tablelands and rolling on into the city. Everything seemed so big and different from my home town. And the coliseum . . . was that just about the biggest thing I had ever seen? I think so. And Tiny's motor cavalcade, all those apple-painted cars pulling into the parking lot one by one . . . was that just about the first time I realized my brother was a celebrity? I think so.

Who could have thought then that one day, years later, I would be standing out in front of the Seattle Center Opera House meeting my famous brother who would once again escort me front row center to hear his beloved country music? No one, I guess. We never know where dreams will take us.

In time, Seattle, too, became Tiny's town and play-ground, because, as it turned out, he didn't belong just to eastern Washington, but to all of Washington State, Seattle included.

It became commonplace for the Tiny entourage, with Dick's Cadillac riding point, to rapidly wind its way over the mountains to its toe-tapping destination: country music in the Opera House.

Dick loved music, but it had to be country! Nothing else would do. Consequently, thousands of customers were given no choice when they stopped at Tiny's, They got Muzak, "Tiny" style. The tunes of Hank Snow, Sonny James, Faron Young, Marty Robbins, The Statler Brothers and Jim Reeves were what smote the ear.

Dick was fiercely loyal to country music and its stars. Any suggestion that another musical style might be nice, for variety, was dismissed with a curt, "No, dammit, this is my business and I'll run it my way. If people don't like it, they don't have to stay." End of discussion.

Actually, the music was right. Tiny's without country music would not have been Tiny's. The stand was such a personal reflection of what Dick was that it just had to be. He had created the business with that flamboyant, "I'll-do-it-my-way" attitude. It was what made Tiny's unique. So like it or not, country music it was.

His love for country music led him to bring some of the biggest names in the country music field to Cashmere. Dick arranged for Hank Snow, Sonny James, Grandpa Jones, Waylon Jennings, and others to give their shows in his hometown and saw to it that proceeds from the performances went to the Cashmere Bulldog Booster Club. After being treated like royalty and feasting at a Tiny-orchestrated banquet, the entertainers continued to Seattle, their next stop.

Cashmere was the smallest stop on tour, but probably the one with the biggest "to do". It never occurred to Dick that he couldn't do anything he wanted. He was an idea person and if it was his idea and he was on fire about it, you could bet he would make it happen.

Dick customarily reserved the middle front row seats

at the Seattle Opera House to see his beloved country entertainers, then proceeded to make the Cashmere Connection an integral part of each show that brought country singers to Seattle.

Never one to miss an advertising opportunity, he made certain that as many "Tiny" cars as possible made the trek to Seattle, parking them in the most visible spot along Mercer Street across from the Opera House. There they sat, working while he was playing . . . apple after apple after apple.

A part of the going-to-the-concert ritual was to have delivered backstage cases of cider, apples, and Aplets and Cotlets (the sugary Cashmere confection Dick was to help make famous). In this milieu, however, Dick would avoid the limelight. He just wanted to do something nice for the folks who sang.

Not content with the advertising value of his string of parked cars on Mercer Street, Dick always bought a full page ad in the concert programs, with which he greeted his Westside constituents. His message was folksy, down home stuff, but it wasn't phoney. It simply reflected the way he was.

Dick's natural manner was a large part of his charm and his success. He was just folks, and that trait came across loudly and clearly in everything he did, especially in the country music area. Many people remember him for that alone. He was small town, howdy, how ya doin', genuine country.

Take it or leave it. The beat he marched to worked for him. It became part of the legend and it played well . . . he probably hummed a few tunes on the way to the bank.

As time went on people began to realize that Tiny was the biggest drawing card that Cashmere had. Bigger than Aplets.

He was better known, you know. He stood out. People recognized him and he did so many things for the school and the community. The western shows, and raising money and turning it over to good causes. He set up the Booster Club.

Later, after he was gone, people would come in and ask, "Where's Tiny?" A lot of them didn't know. They still come in and say "Where's Tiny's stand." All these years later. —RON DOANE

But his music and all that. Every time I hear Jim Reeves, I think of Dick. "Four Walls", I'll never forget "Four Walls". "Four walls to hear me, four walls to see . . ." Dick would sing it as loud as he could sing it. —NOLA HENSLEY

I did cooler work. That's real funny because I'd be sitting there in my down jacket filling up all these little baskets with peaches and cherries and you could always tell when someone had squeezed the peaches. Dick would burst into the cooler and his face would be just bright red. He'd sit down on a couple of those boxes of cider and just try to calm himself. That's when he would say, "Why do I get so upset? Even though I have the signs there, I know they're going to squeeze the peaches. Why do I get so upset?" —SCOTT GREEN

My grandma, Inez Simpson, made Dick's shirts and he'd take Grandma shopping and the two of them would go and she'd come back with bolts of yardage. I don't remember how much yardage it took but it took quite a bit. And she made some of his Bermuda shorts, too, and he'd get some of the flashiest colors I've ever seen. —NOLA HENSLEY

40

Tiny, the Cider King, models his trademarks, a gallon jug of cider, casual sports shirt and plaid shorts — sizes: extra, extra large.

Neither the mountains nor the town of Cashmere could dwarf Tiny's last fruit st
the 'Fifties and 'Sixties.

of the nation's largest. The stand was a Cashmere Valley landmark during

The signs, nailed up by the thousands all over the Northwest, drew the tourist toward Cashmere and as they drew closer, the signs got larger.

If it had four wheels and he owned it, Tiny painted it. He gave the author a new car, but there was a price — it had to be painted with the Tiny logo.

9

THE MELTING POT

From Armenia, an ocean and a continent away,
two immigrants named Tertsagian and Balaban
brought to the United States
an old world recipe for Turkish Delight,
which the good candy makers transformed
into the Washington confection known as Aplets and Cotlets.
When Armenian met German-Irish,
the melting pot began to cook up more than candy.

Aplets!" When I was young, our favorite treat was the box of Aplets and Cotlets Dad brought home as part of the family Christmas tradition.

"Just take one. Make them last," was Mom's futile admonishment as we dived into a box of tempting powdered sugar-coated candies. Her other lesson, "Never take the last one", evidently didn't make much of an impression, either, since a request to have one more often turned up an empty box. Somebody had taken it!

These were products unique to the world and dear to the hearts of all who lived in Cashmere. Aplets, made with a blending of apples and walnuts, and Cotlets (apricots and walnuts), not only helped make Cashmere famous, they

41

also were important economically for they comprised another market for the surpluses of fruit grown in both normal and bumper years.

Swans, angels and stars — gauzy ethereal creations — were among my first memories of Aplets and Cotlets from my curbside, lowside view as the float from Cashmere's Liberty Orchards wafted by. We waited anxiously for it to ease into view and were never disappointed. A perennial star of the Wenatchee Apple Blossom Festival.

"Here comes the Aplet float," became a rolling murmur as spectators craning for a first glimpse blocked one another's vision. Bent at ninety degree angles, people sitting on the curb or in chairs leaned streetward while standees stretched to their tip-toed tallest to capture the moment.

"Did they do it? Did they win Grand Sweepstakes again?" Usually.

To me, the fantasy-like themes and soft, dreamy silks and satins of the angels seemed like heaven. Children suspended on make-believe clouds appeared to float above the street. I dreamed that one day I would be one of the little girls who rode on those clouds.

For children, Liberty Orchards had created magic; for adults, one more reason to be proud. We were from Cashmere. We had something special. Our town was known for its famous candy company, the one that brought "oohs" and "aahs" when its latest creation glided slowly, gracefully down the avenue.

It sticks. It fills the memory of childhood because childhood's the time when all is brand-new special, bigger than life. Fresh. Youthful innocence is not yet cluttered with the "I-dare-you-to-impress-me" attitude which comes with age. The mind's eye of a child is a wondrous thing with its easy entry into the playland of imagination. Someone at the Aplet plant must have understood that child's-eye view because they took us there every year at Apple Blossom Time. Do you suppose they had some children working for them?

With Aplet management, quality came first. Reward was the logical consequence. I loved their floats, their candy and the fact that they were from my hometown. Provincialism. I can't help it. I have powdered sugar in my blood.

Those were pre-Tiny days.

* * * *

Liberty Orchards grew from a small confectionery and became a big business and the pride of Cashmere long before my brother began to spend thousands of dollars advertising their product and much of each summer introducing this unique Northwest candy to myriad travelers from across the United States and Canada:

"I'm from Cashmere. That's where they make Aplets and Cotlets." In time, the standard community braggadocio—the Aplet Connection—had to make room for a variation:

"I'm from Cashmere. That's where Tiny's is." We hadn't an inkling then that one day the fruit candy would become an important part of our family livelihood. It was much later that Tiny would introduce, promote, and sell it in volumes limited only by his imagination, and Liberty Orchards' productive capacity, vision and willingness to extend credit.

Dick's enormous orders made the candy makers extremely nervous. In the beginning Tiny's account with Liberty tended more to the debit side than the credit. Fortunately for both parties, "Tiny's" and "Aplets" was to prove a coupling of a unique product with a unique promoter. They knew how to make candy; Dick knew how to sell it.

A second generation of management at Liberty Orchards now consisted of John Chakirian, Balaban's nephew, and Tertsagian's son-in-law, Dick Odabashian. Two gentlemen combining old world charm with astute business sense.

Innovation was the driving force as the two firms expanded together. As Dick Graves' fertile mind generated new ideas for marketing Aplets and Cotlets in his business, Odabashian and Chakirian had the foresight and the nerve to go along with him. The result was success, sweet success.

Astute businessmen, Odabashian and Chakirian realized that the impetuous young giant who frequently barged into their offices was an unstoppable entrepreneur, a rare talent. This man was a promoter with a vision of what a fruit stand should be and Aplets was a part of it. This was the place. This was the product. Let's sell it!

Along the way Dick Graves challenged their conservative business sense, their patience and their accounts receivable. He was a risk. He proposed doing things never before done and in order to do them he needed candy—lots of candy for those elaborate displays that would become a Tiny's trademark years before the technique became the "taught" thing to do.

Tiny's ideas worked and the Fruit Stand/Candy Factory Connection grew from a tenuous beginning to a success story that, according to Odabashian, has yet to be equalled. He believes that "Tiny's Fruit Stand" retains its standing as the world's largest single retail outlet for Aplets and Cotlets.

There were heady days ahead when Aplets and Cotlets would become synonymous with "Tiny's" and customers would ask if he made the candy himself, but first came years of hard work, innovation and selling. It wasn't so easy early on. It never is.

Tiny had an interesting way of hiring employees. He went to all the Cashmere football games and hired the boys who hustled on the field. He knew they would hustle at the stand and they did. As a result, the customers were pleased at the service and entertained by the swiftness with which it was carried out. Tiny loved all his employees and rewarded them appropriately for their loyalty and their response to his demands.

—BILL TARVER

I'll never forget one time he came in and you remember how he used to sweat? It was just running off of him. And he took a watermelon and dropped it and just gouged it out and ate that thing. I thought, "My God, I couldn't stand all that sticky stuff on me!" When it was a hundred degrees, Dick would go back in that cooler, where it was freezing, and there he was sweating. He'd sit on those racks of cider, no shirt. He'd get so hot, he'd take it off. —NOLA HENSLEY

One time he brought the car in and wanted it painted and lettered in time for the Apple Blossom Festival. When he came in and it it wasn't ready, he got mad, went out and slammed the door so hard it loosened one of those bricks. He called right away and apologized. We had it ready the morning of the festival. —PETE MATSON

I'd go down and pick up Ken and Dick would take me to his office and we would talk about finances and his worries about finances. I'm sure Dick Odabashian and Aplets worried about him, too, but Dick (Odabashian) once told me, "He was the biggest outlet we've ever had." He'd sell us, you know, a dozen boxes and say, "If you could sell them like Tiny does, we'd have it made." —RON DOANE

45

10

A BURR UNDER THE SADDLE

There have been changes over the years
at the Aplet factory
and Tiny was instrumental
in making some of them happen.
He never had anything to do with making the candy,
but, my oh my, he had much to do with selling it.

Tiny was a natural, knowing instinctively what would work for him. It was his "Tiny touch".

A new marketing technique was taking shape in Dick's mind. He observed that many people wouldn't buy a new candy product without first tasting it. He concluded we could sell more if we offered customers a taste test. No sooner had he come to this conclusion than Tiny's began offering samples. An expensive gesture.

"Dammit! Dick would grouse. "We have to have factory samples. We can't continue like this. It's eating up al the profits."

Having decided this, he appointed himself an irritant of one, a burr under the Odabashian saddle, to persuade

46

Aplets and Cotlets to include samples in their merchandising program. Off to the plant he charged with the pronouncement, only to meet with rejection. According to Odabashian, the company simply was not set up then for that kind of promotion. Therefore, the answer was "No".

Dick Graves was not pleased. He replied, "If you want us to sell your damn candy, then we will have to have samples," and stalked off.

On returning to the stand, Dick instructed us to continue opening boxes of candy as we needed them while also keeping track of how many we used. He would record how much was sold. His expectations were confirmed; when samples were offered, sales zoomed.

Back to the factory. This time Dick had two mandates for the businessmen at Liberty Orchards. One was a repeat: "If you want us to sell your damn candy, we will have to have samples." The other: "I expect to be reimbursed for the candy we have already used." I wasn't there, but it was my understanding that a robust exchange of opinions ensued. Deadlock. Liberty Orchards' view was, "We can't make money if we give the candy away." Dick's view was, "You'll make more if you do." A compromise. How about using the trimmings from candy cut for packaging? A good mutual solution. Everyone was happy. Tiny could have samples and Liberty Orchards could make good use of the excess. This sounds like an ending, but it was actually a beginning.

We were using samples, available only when a new batch was cooked, faster than the factory was able to supply them. Dick called announcing we needed more. Their question was, "What are you doing with the ones we gave you?"

The rather cocky reply followed, "Selling your damn candy!" But that was, after all, the point. Off to the plant again. This time he didn't have to tell them what he wanted. They knew.

There appeared to be only one answer. Make candy for the sole purpose of sampling. It is to be remembered as a major breakthrough for Tiny's and for Liberty Orchards. The company's understanding of the effectiveness of the taste test on a grand scale (it was already a part of the plant tour) coupled with their willingness to take a risk with Tiny was to prove financially beneficial. From that stage when trimmings were used for samples to the next one when pieces were prepared for small individual paper cups and eventually displayed in plastic trays and self-help containers, the idea of sampling has paid for itself many times over. The idea worked.

Henceforth, a stop at Tiny's meant a taste of Aplets, an integral component of the personal greeting. I know. I delivered such a greeting thousands of times.

"Would you care for a sample of an Aplet or Cotlet while you look around? This candy is made right here in Cashmere from the fresh pulp and juice of the apple or apricot and mixed with fresh English walnuts. Now make yourself at home. Browse all you like. If you need any help, just let us know." Actually there wasn't much hard sell involved. The candy sold itself once people had the opportunity to taste. It was good. It still is!

As Dicks' imagination grew along with the business, so did his view of what was possible. He regularly gave stress to his friends at the factory, particularly Ben Schadler, the plant manager. A common scenario:

"Hello, Ben. This is Tiny. Could you send over 30 Aplets, 30 Cotlets, 30 of the combination and 10 of the bars?"

"Great!"

Not great . . .

"What's this, Ben?"

"It's your order."

"It's not my order."

"Well, it certainly is. You ordered 100 boxes of candy."

"Boxes, hell, Ben. I meant cases."

"Cases? What are you going to do with 100 cases?"

"What do you think I'm going to do with them. Sell them!"

"We don't have that many cooked."

"Then cook!"

And so it went. They cooked. He sold.

Displays were enormous. Twenty-foot tables made just for Aplets and Cotlets held hundreds of the pink and yellow boxes. Displays were thrown up quickly and spontaneously. In a matter of minutes Tiny could rotate stock, open cases and build a new creation. With his big fist, he would pop open the seal on the case, then tip it upside down, spreading the boxes on the table. All of this was seemingly in one motion.

Bang! Rip! Voila! Some of us struggled more. I tried the fist routine. Thud! Ouch! Pain! "Where's the boxcutter?" Dick knew all the tricks. He sensed people were hesitant to touch things if they thought they were ruining the order. He wanted it neat, but not too neat. After building the perfect arrangement, he then created a calculated mess making the display "touchable".

Row on row of boxes now circled the two-tiered tables, leaning on one another like collapsed dominos. Tiny, removing some of the boxes from each of the rows, two here, three there, six on the corner, put the finishing touches on his planned disarray. Setting those diagonally on top of the others, he randomly placed three facing one way, two facing another, creating the effect around the table that many had already been sold. Because the arrangement was imperfect, customers selected readily from either top or bottom.

In a sense it was, ironically, a perfect display. The volume and placement said "Take me." Customers did.

Often two or three boxes at a time. We were intrigued by the phenomenon. The more sales there appeared to have been, the more we sold. The effect was magnetic and lucrative.

Of course, there would come a point at which each display needed "sweetening". Never fear, Tiny was ready with the new order, probably larger than the last. He was on to something!

Dick taught us how to build the displays, too, although we never did it quite the same. He might say something like, "That looks good, maybe a little too neat." At that point he would make his patented "Tiny" mess.

He had other tricks. "Hand them a box of candy. If you can just get people to hold one, they probably won't put it back down." He was right. It was fun. Behind that jovial disposition and those twinkly eyes was a businessman who was intent on earning a buck. He was good at it.

Dick's marketing sense was instrumental in bringing about other changes. He realized there was a niche for a form of packaging that was not as fancy or as expensive as the boxed candy. Families did not need the gift boxes for themselves since it all tasted the same inside, anyway. He thought, why not sell the candy bars in packages? Pack them six Aplets, six Cotlets, convenient for travelers. Another call to the plant. Another likely scenario:

"Hello, Ben. This is Tiny. I need a couple thousand Aplet and Cotlet bars."

"Now, Tiny, you know we don't have that kind of inventory in bars.

We'll have to cook. When do you want them?"

"You're right and now!"

Poor Ben.

The bags of bars were a hit. Part of the success was their affordability and another was the huge display. He covered two tables with hundreds of the bags of bars . . .

50

mountain bars! It always worked. The more there was of a product the more it sold. Volume sold volume. He knew no other way. It became part of the Tiny legend.

Not one to miss an opportunity to advertise, he inserted an order form inside each bag with prices and postage on one side and on the other, always "face" up . . . that smiling Tiny. If the folks from Council Bluffs, Iowa, or Kankakee, Illinois, ate the candy before returning home — as they inevitably would — they could order more and he was there to remind them. Clever, that Tiny.

Another innovation inspired by Dick Graves was the packaging of Aplets and Cotlets in bulk form. Just as the candy bars had been a success, Dick felt that the trimmings would sell as well. They tried it. It worked. Bulk candy displayed in the expansive Tiny fashion was an instant hit. A surprising thing happened. People bought even more: the now quite affordable and convenient forms for themselves and the fancy gift boxes for others. Bulk packaging is a part of the company's marketing strategy still.

In those years Tiny's introduced thousands of new customers from the four corners of the United States and Canada to the Northwest confection from Cashmere. He made money. Liberty Orchards made money. We all worked hard striving to top sales of the year before. In the walk-in cooler Dick kept a wall chart comparing yearly totals. Each week it was updated. Each week we topped the previous records. Dick's enthusiasm and his own sales acumen were infectious.

Our motto became: "Everyone goes out with Aplets." It was fun. Success breeds success. Those were very happy days.

One was especially happy for me. Although I never rode the Aplet float, I had the good fortune to do even better. I received the red carpet treatment and floated on the clouds in real life. Dick Odabashian, a veteran pilot and at that time sales director for the company, flew his own

51

plane around the country to do business for Liberty Orchards. For a reward at the end of a successful "Aplet season", Odabashian flew several of us to Seattle for dinner one evening.

At a time when my world was not much larger than the Cashmere Valley, this was pretty heady stuff. On arriving at Boeing Field, we had no need of rented transportation. Our host had his own car at the airport. I was impressed. We were whisked off to the "Red Carpet" restaurant where Mr. Odabashian was greeted on a first name basis and we were treated royally.

It was a thrill . . . lots better than a float. This was the real thing. I was even higher than the clouds and the red carpet was a bonus.

Those were good times, sunny days for all of us. The Aplet-Cotlet connection was very sweet, made even sweeter with a few "Tiny" changes.

By the way, would you care for a sample of an Aplet or a Cotlet?

One summer, Harold and I needed some money and I saw Dick and I said, "Do you need any help?" He asked me what I did. I said, "Dick, I don't know. I haven't worked, outside of raising two boys." He said, "Come on down and I'll put you to work in the kitchen." I had no idea what I was going to get into.

I'd come to work about seven to seven-thirty in the morning. I'd walk into the kitchen and there he was with his cleaver and in his Bermuda shorts. And the sweat running off of him. Slicing onions, tears running down his eyes. Onions and tomatoes. No one could slice those the way he wanted them. He wanted them cut just right. Nobody touched those. —NOLA HENSLEY

11

BRINGING UP THE REAR

Walking a tightrope is precarious
Skating on thin ice is treacherous.
Flying on the trapeze is perilous . . .
but other, unexpected, situations can arise
which also balance one on the edge of terror,
flirting with the unspeakable.
Sometimes one person's horror is another person's delight.
The humor is a matter of perspective. You decide.

I remember most days at the stand primarily in terms of long hours of hard work, but a few things happened to break the monotony and stuck with me because of their absurdities. Take what happened one fall day when Dick and I were working together, he mingling with the customers and passing out samples of apples which he had dramatically cut into slices with a large butcher knife, I going about my mundane tasks.

Like a carnival pitchman, Dick had an eye-catching routine. As unsuspecting customers inspected the fruit, they would look up, startled to see Dick looming high over them. Whereupon, Dick would proceed to mesmerize them by skillfully retrieving the knife from his back pocket where it pointedly protruded. With practiced dexterity he would quickly crack-slice-twist apples into halves and then again into quarters.

"Care for a taste?" he would inquire, charmingly. Once hearts had receded from throats, the answer usually was, "Yes." This flamboyant technique almost always brought results in the form of sales, but, then, four-hundred pounds of human being wielding a butcher knife in one hand while offering apples in the other had to have been difficult to refuse. You know . . . keep the giant friendly.

His act was impressive and Dick loved the show as much as his customers did. On one particular day, however, he gave more of a show than he had planned.

It was Dick's custom to walk by the checkstand and announce what I was to ring up on the cash register. If the sale included a box of apples, it was also his custom to lift the forty-pound box, balance it on the flat of one hand and boost it high in the air. Apples and ham! Atlas and the world.

But that time, as he waltzed by the checkstand, he proclaimed, "Two boxes!" Cute. He had both boxes overhead. The bystanders were goggle-eyed.

So was I. While the onlookers oohed and aahed about his strength, I casually began ringing up the sales and packaging other items they were purchasing. In the midst of the transaction, I heard him bellow:

"SHARON!"

"What?" I blithely responded.

With considerable increase in intensity, Dick roared, "Don't just stand there saying 'what' . . . GET THE HELL OUT HERE!"

I'm clever. I knew he meant I should move with haste.

And what to my wondering eyes should appear? . . . my brother in a most compromising situation. It seems the big show-off had not anticipated that raising both hands above one's head causes one's stomach to retreat from the confines of one's waistband. His pants were rapidly responding to the law of gravity and it was obvious I was to save him from red-faced, bare-bottomed embarassment.

For a split second I was deliciously tempted not to negate the natural forces of nature; however, I valued my life, my job, and my brother's right to some modesty. To his relief, I arrived just in time to grab the back of his belt and deny the tourists a display of his ample derriere.

It was a memorable scene. I'm sure those who witnessed the show never forgot Tiny marching across the parking lot, boxes of apples overhead, being trailed by a hysterical helper holding up his pants.

I think he modified his act after that. Too bad! The customers loved it!

Mid-July through most of August we made those little trips to the canal to swim (see Chapter 12). Nobody wanted to be the driver because Dick and the rest of the crew would sit in the back with the tailgate down. So you got a full load back there and he always wanted to be dropped off at Masevner's.

Well, as you come up to get onto the canal road it's a steep enough of a pitch that just as you start up, you completely lose everything. You don't see and you know that you have to turn hard enough to the right or you'll drop off. It makes you a nervous wreck because you are coming up on the ditch and you gotta crank it hard to the right so that you don't go into the ditch. If you crank too early you're gonna drop your right rear tire.

One time I came real close to dropping that right rear tire and I had to gun it and almost flipped them out the back. It was the proverbial "you're caught between a rock and a hard spot". That was probably the hardest thing I ever did in the four or five years I worked there. It was mental pressure like you couldn't believe.

—SCOTT GREEN, employee at Tiny's Fruit Stand

55

12

OLE SWIMMIN' HOLE WITH A TWIST

What's normal? Don't ask me.
None of my adventures with Tiny were normal
and some were bizarre.

The most amazing aspect of Dick's escapades was that after a while they didn't seem weird, such as his daily dunk in the irrigation canal. The first time I went with him I was thunderstruck by the drama that unfolded and I cringe when I think of it. Later what he did seemed normal. I got used to it.

That day was a scorcher. We all were hot. Dick, the hottest, had the coolest ways to find relief. One was the swim in the canal. He said, "Sharon, I'll go get my swim trunks on and you meet me at the back door with the pick-up." I should never have gotten into the driver's seat, but I did so, with misgivings, knowing the seat was all the way back and my legs probably too short to reach the pedals without stretching. My misgivings were well justified. I started the engine. Manipulating clutch and gas pedal clumsily, with the tips of my toes, I started the truck in reverse. Coming to life suddenly, the truck threw me forward with a lurch then, as I shifted to low, backward like a bucking bronco coming out of the chute.

Dick was waiting impatiently (the only way he ever waited), as my unruly charge and I shot around the corner into view.

Leap! Stop! Leap! Stop! I had little control. Dick had less. He was convulsed with laughter. I insisted I couldn't drive the truck. I don't know why I insisted. He wasn't blind. He ignored me. "This," he said, "will be fun." Warped sense of humor.

Dick, now an eye-popping sight in his swim trunks, plunked himself onto the bed of the pick-up, legs dangling. His two German Shepherds, Simba and Bimba, whom he had invited on this outing, joined him like two furry bookends. Now, the trio's combined heft tilted the front of the truck skyward just enough to make my visibility even more marginal.

Nose up, tail down, we headed out. Back toward the fruit stand we shot, with Dick laughing, dogs barking, and sister screaming. Around to the front we lurched. Oh, fine! Now we were going to make a public spectacle of ourselves.

Our customers and fellow employees — all sober, normal people — were treated to a strange apparition: a bucking truck, one oversize passenger, two barking dogs and a terrified driver who, for what her legs contributed to her prowess as a pickup driver may as well have been born without them.

Leap! Stop! Bark! Bark! Leap! Stop! Bark! Bark!

We must have been a sight.

We came to the crucial stage of our outing, the crossing of four lanes of Highway 2 at a dangerous intersection — no easy task under normal circumstances. Normalcy never even entered the picture. Lunacy ruled.

"Dick, I can't drive this thing across the highway. We'll be killed." Hysterical laughter. "No we won't. Just be ready when I tell you. Then really romp on it."

I should have been paralyzed with fear, but I already had no control.

Fear wouldn't have helped.

"OK, Sharon, it's clear. GO!"

I didn't even look. I just slid down in the seat, slammed my foot against the gas pedal and chinned myself on the steering wheel. There is no logical reason why I should have reached the other side with brother and two dogs intact. We spurted across the highway like a turbo-fired roadrunner. Dick loved it. So did the dogs. Laughter and barking followed me as we tore across and careened up the country road to the canal.

From my perch, peering over the dash, I attempted to respond as Dick shouted directions:

"Just drive up here. Don't cross the bridge. Make a sharp right." "Are you kidding me? I'll drive into the canal."

"No, you won't. I'll tell you when to turn."

From my worm's-eye perspective, there was neither ditch nor road, only the hood of Dick's ridiculous truck, now listing badly to one side from the slant of the road and the combined weight of its payload.

Sharp right? This was crazy. There was no way this feat could be accomplished. Ninety-degree turns were for drill teams, not for trucks being guided by remote control. I could just see it. Leap! No stop!

Glub! "Dick, you do it."

"Come on, Sharon!" he snapped. "We don't have time to waste. I have to get back to the stand." The fake, angry routine. It worked every time.

"All right."

"O.K., go forward just a little. That's good. NOW! TURN!"

58

As he gave the directions, the truck and I responded.

Forward! Leap, for God's sake! Adrenalin! Terror! Turn!

We made it! I don't know how. I was weak. My legs were shaking. No one seemed to notice, neither dog, nor brother.

My passengers tumbled out, lowering the nose of the truck by several inches. Good, this might help me to see through the steering wheel to the narrow ditch road I was supposed to keep this fitful critter on. I didn't like what I saw. The ditch threatened on one side; the bank on the other.

Before I could re-panic the show started.

Into the canal sailed the two barking, whining dogs. Obviously this was a doggie treat. Water flew! The barking and splashing was followed by frantic clawing at the edges of the canal as the dogs exited and vanished into the orchard.

While this was happening, "Flipper", was positioning himself for his own patented plunge into the canal. Standing on the bridge, back to the canal, Dick catapulted his hugeness into the water, seat first. The dogs had not cornered the market on the big splash. A wall of water surrounded him on all sides. I think it's called displacement.

To watch him splash and swim and fight the current was a joy. Tiny was in his element. He was relaxed. He was having a lark. He was Water Baby!

As soon as the dogs heard his gigantic splash, they raced back and hurled themselves into the drink with him. They splashed in and climbed out repeatedly as Tiny, the Cider King, bobbed down the ditch, sometimes floating on his back, sometimes swimming, sometimes standing up against the surging current. As he played and burbled, I drove precariously alongside.

Leap! Stop! Leap! Stop! Practice hadn't helped. Just

when I thought we had established a pattern of leaping, stopping, and swimming, Dick pulled a new trick. Standing up in the ditch next to a board which had been placed across it, he reached up and pulled down a bottle of shampoo. Of course! Doesn't everyone keep his grooming needs on a plank in the middle of someone else's orchard?

After lathering up what little hair he had on his crew-cut head, he dunked and gurgled, dunked and gurgled. Good, all was rinsed. On we went.

Leap! Stop! Leap! Stop!

What next? By now I suspected there would be a next. Sure enough, there was. On the next plank, waiting patiently, was a bar of soap. Same scene. Different parts. It was classic Tiny. At this point a rubber ducky wouldn't have surprised me.

Was there a message there? I think so. A "Tiny's" isn't created by someone who doesn't float down canals to shampoo and soap. That person would be too normal.

The cold water must have brought him to his senses. He drove home.

The integrity and the honesty. They (his kids) were taught never to take tips, to treat everybody with "Ma'm or Sir". Things that the parents would tell them they wouldn't pay any attention, but coming from Dick they really accepted it. I think in a lot of cases it shaped their future.
—RON DOANE

When we finished the signs on the front of the building . . . God, he was proud of it! It was beautiful. We had the neon around that huge red apple. That was eighteen feet high. And the big hamburger and milkshake and the Aplet and Cotlet boxes. The sign across the front was 300 feet long.
—PETE MATSON

13

PEACHES IN A PINCH

If thee values thy life,
thee doest not break one of the Tiny Commandments:
"Thou shalt not pinch the peaches".

T he customer is always right! You're not paid to question what they do. You are paid to make them feel welcome, give them good service and be polite. No matter what, remember you don't have the right to talk back to the customer, even though you may feel like it. Understand?"

"Yes."

Not only did we understand, we obeyed. Four-hundred pounds of temper is incredibly intimidating. We minded our manners, trying hard to make people feel welcome and to give them the kind of service that Tiny's had become known for.

Only one person on the staff was brave enough to

ignore the admonishment to be nice to customers, no matter what. He was one of our permanent employees, had been a part of the Tiny saga from its inception, was about six-feet three-inches tall and weighed four-hundred pounds.

Tiny's habit of making an exception to his own rules made for great drama. One incident, in particular, clings vividly to my memory. It was a busy day and Dick and I were working together at the checkstand, ringing up sales on the cash registers.

Back to back, we had different perspectives. Dick had a clear view of the refrigerated fruit display. Looking in the opposite direction toward the hamburger stand and patio, I was unaware of the irritation that was about to cause a pre-Mt St. Helen's eruption. However, as soon as I heard him mutter a few words through gritted teeth, I knew all hell was about to break loose. (I hated the tension, but loved the drama. Trouble was a-brewin!).

I sized up the situation at a glance. Dick had seen in the mirror over the display case the reflection of a woman's busy hand picking up, pinching and putting back in the baskets some beautiful big Red Haven peaches — not a good idea. Dick took great pride in the fruit put out for display and he knew from painful experience that each time the customer pinched a peach she left an ugly bruise. As far as eye appeal was concerned, the peaches were ruined. They had to be replaced.

Dick delivered his first warning in a controlled voice with polite authority.

"Lady, those peaches are ripe." I turned to capture in an instant the unfolding mini-drama. Oh no! She was still pinching. Double jeopardy.

If Dick disliked bruised peaches with a passion, he hated being disobeyed even more. This customer was out of line and something told me she was going to hear about it. Glee! This was going to be good. I really loved it when he went against his sacred "the customer is always right" rule.

Vicarious revenge.

I sneaked another peek. Pinch! Pinch! Pinch!

Tension.

Like a cat that knew she had nine lives, the lady continued her peach mutilations oblivious to the danger.

Hey! There was no way I was going to miss this. All work stopped and the customers, sensing excitement, joined me in watching speechless as Tiny propelled his bulk from checkstand to display case in three giant steps. Picking up one of the Red Havens in his huge hand, he squeezed the peach with all the force his strength and anger could muster. The lady didn't have a chance. Neither did the peach. Peach pulp splattered everywhere: onto the mirror, on Tiny and all over the lady. Staring with disbelief, she began backing toward her car. Tiny followed, shaking his fruit-filled fist, while slowly, pointedly and very angrily repeating, "You see, lady . . . these peaches are ripe!" Somewhere in those action filled seconds, she lost her desire for Red Haven peaches, ripe or otherwise. So much for peaches and cream for breakfast, not to mention the cultivation of a return customer.

Later that year Dick came up with a bizarre remedy for the fruit pinching problem. When Italian prunes ripened later in the summer, he filled a large section of the display case with them. (If you know Italian prunes, you know they are firm little fruits!) After finishing an elaborate display, he placed (with revenge in his heart and michief in his eye) a sign on the prunes which read, "You can pinch the hell out of these!"

"When I think of him, I think of the shyness in his smile."
—DIANA ROBINSON

14

THE LITTLE STAND GROWS UP

Time passes, slips away and change comes,
sometimes so gradually it goes undetected,
at other times so abruptly
it shakes our sense of reality,
grabs our attention and demands action.
Such was the case with Tiny's
Fruit Stand in the late '50's.

Having played "fruit stand" up and down Highway 2 between Cashmere and Peshastin/Dryden, Tiny had established himself as King of the Road, at least that particular stretch of road. Things were going well. He had become Mr. Eastern Washington, the man with the signs, the man to see.

Business was good. Dick had dreams of a chain of fruit stands up and down the coast, soon but not yet. If that were to happen, it would have to wait until it was financially feasible. For now he would concentrate on what he had. The best laid plans . . .

When Dick discovered that the highway department was planning a new four-lane highway on the north side of the Wenatchee river, a complete bypass of Cashmere, he knew this signalled a potentially devastating change in his current operation. In its present location, Tiny's, for all intents and purposes, would be out of business.

What to do? Even his trail of signs couldn't coax enough people that far off the main road to keep the business profitable. This was a complicated dilemma, one which would have to be solved if Tiny's was to continue to exist.

The big earth eaters growling and clawing their way through the hill across the river were cutting out more than a path for speedy stretches of highway. They were cutting the heart out of Tiny's Fruit Stand. Not unlike the stubborn mountain of shale that continued to slough off even after the job seemed finished, Tiny, a stubborn mountain of determination, managed to come back even after it appeared he was finished.

Not surprisingly, Dick cast prudence to the winds and chose to go heavily into debt in order to purchase highway frontage property and build a new stand. With the help of Dick Odabashion, who financed the property, and Liberty Orchards which gave financial backing, Dick Graves was able to relocate and "start again".

And what a start it was! Deciding to put all his apples in one box, Tiny proceeded to build the stand of his dreams. Out of the starting gate some things were given. The stand would be big. It would be colorful. It would be beautiful. Pure Tiny. All Northwest. Only in Cashmere.

Happily, it was to become the stand by which all others would be measured. As much as it was Tiny's, it was also ours. By the 1960's Tiny's was a popular landmark. For some it was much more, a part of a pattern. For them, travel through Eastern Washington included a stop at Tiny's. Washingtonians and Pacific Northwesterners had a personal as well as a monetary investment in the Tiny phenomenon. Tiny's was their place, too, a part of the contemporary culture.

By correctly anticipating his customers would return again and again, Tiny found the risk of expansion less frightening. In a real sense, his increasing horde of loyal customers helped the big guy build his big stand. He appreciated the patronage. When Dick Graves put up the tall sign at the parking lot exit which read, "Thank's, Folks!", he meant it.

Tiny's Fruit Stand didn't just happen. It was planned, down to the most minute detail. Detail made the difference. Dick's free-wheeling enterprise was successful because he was able to combine in one person the grandiose ideas of a visionary with the down-to-earth practicalities of a builder and businessman.

Thinking of it now, I imagine his brain must have been racing at maximum RPM. Considering the gargantuan task of planning a new stand together with the exciting opportunity to do it as he really wanted it done, it's a wonder Dick ever got any sleep. I came to understand how his mind worked. One idea exploded onto another and another like a starburst.

But he managed and the result was a finely tuned roadside vending machine, running at peak performance twenty-four hours a day, nine months out of the year. With a huge financial investment, creditors at the door, and a voracious business demanding huge volumes of product, Tiny was under tremendous pressure to make the new stand profitable.

The cautious thing to do would have been to cut back on his vision, but he didn't. He went all out and in the process attended to detail, the formula which had worked so well for him in the past. Tiny's attention to minutiae blended to create a single impression. Although it may not have seemed like it to the observer, everything had a purpose and a way to be done. His way. His purpose. His dream.

One detail was obvious: the simple wooden signs populating the roadsides of the northwest states, signs that were to lead people to Tiny's in the first place.

"Blue and white. It shows up best. It looks neat. The larger signs should be red, white and blue, highlighted with yellow. We need to keep them simple, just a few words. Easier to read from the car. We need to place them so that people will see them just as they come around the corner. Put them up high, so they are harder to tear down."

Always he had a reason for what he did.

The more signs he put up the more people came. The gimmick fed on itself: more people, more signs, more people. A map on the wall beside his desk marked the spots where signs had been placed. Hundreds of straight pins with red, white or blue heads stood out in pointed declaration of a sign of the times. These were symbolic of Tiny's time in the Northwest — signs of the signs, which more than any other factor contributed to his becoming a legend.

Each winter Tiny and Dean Schlecta travelled to the far corners of the Pacific Northwest and beyond to claim the advertising frontier.

Nothing was haphazard, from the big red, white and blue sign which soared over the stand (at the time it was first erected in 1953, it was said to be the largest neon sign in the Northwest) to the bright pink petunias which blanketed its foundation with a riot of color. Something as seemingly simple as the flags which waved happily from the roof and the access road were all a part of the circus which played in his mind. They were typical of the expensive extras which he felt were necessary. The flags weathered and had to be replaced often, but he suffered the expense willingly. Flags were an integral part of the impression he intended to create.

Detail.

"Welcome to Tiny's." "Thanks, Folks!" Always the little touches. He knew how to use the visual. Pete Matson,

Dick's good friend and his sign painter over most of the years, remembers spending three months working on the new stand. He constructed giant cutouts — milkshake, hamburger, apples — no small task. Installed so as to extend above the roof line, these eight-to-ten-foot-tall creations had to be designed, painted and mounted as only Tiny would have them done.

In addition to the cutouts and the large Tiny logo which had to be painted across the front of the roof facade, there was the blue neon sign to be built and hung to highlight the stand. Everything was a major project because Tiny and Pete were starting from scratch and every piece was equally important.

Pete spent weeks painting the interior. He painted giant pink and white apple blossoms on the interior walls, menus on the walls of the hamburger stand, apples on the front and sides of the checkout stands, "his" and "her" apples for the restrooms, and apples on the toilet seats and lids.

Now, that's detail!

Planters and hanging baskets for the petunias (grown by his friends at Cashmere Floral) . . . waste cans every few feet painted to blend . . . display tables built for the stand and gift shop . . . all part of the plan.

This stand had it all under one roof: a glass enclosed gift shop, storage facilities, walk-in refrigeration room, and Dick's apartment. At the north end of the building was the hamburger stand and patio. Hang the canvass awning that stretched the length of the 300-foot stand and you have an impressive edifice — the one Dick wanted.

Add to this the sawdust floor and "Tiny" and you have the grown-up version of the little stand, all dressed up and ready to go to town. And go to town he did, attending to detail all the way. It was more fun than ever.

Tiny's mind never stopped working. "Next year we'll have more petunias. Next year we'll have monkeys!"

Monkeys? Yes, and chipmunks. Always something.

His attention to detail occasionally brought unanticipated results.

The chipmunks are a case in point. One would predict cute little cages with little wheels would be a chipmunk's delight. Not so. at least not if there are too many chipmunk cousins in one cage.

It seems Dick hadn't done enough research on this bright idea. The morning after the chipmunks had been placed in their new "condo", Dick was appalled to encounter a chipmunk massacre. The poor little things had become so claustrophobic they had attacked one another and bitten off tails, ears and feet. It was an awful sight. So much for the chipmunks.

The monkeys lasted longer, but were a constant souce of problems. It was not uncommon for Dick to get a call from a neighboring orchardist complaining that Tiny's monkeys were out again and the dogs were going crazy. Would Dick get the hell over there and get his monkeys? Expletives flew every time.

"Those damn monkeys are out again!" Tiny would swear. "I'm going to kill the little SOB's!" We were confident he didn't mean it. We knew he had become hooked on them and now thought they were cute. He often could be seen down at the monkey cage, feeding and talking to his little furry friends.

Troublesome they were, and never more so than when they got out. Catching them was next to impossible. It wasn't easy being a monkey papa! I thought the whole thing was a riot. Quite smartly, I had the good sense not to say so.

Dean Slechta, Dick's right hand man, remembers one occasion when one of the monkeys was bounding up and down Wenatchee Avenue. At that point, the show biz side of Dick's nature surfaced. With radio picking up on the nonsense, Dick decided to go with the flow. A little free advertising never hurts. Dean said Dick was at the heighth of his glory. Such ado about monkeys!

Dick was able to pay close attention to crises at the monkey cage because he had installed an elaborate intercom system throughout the stand (another of his important details). Though he might be busy in the checkout stand, he was, in reality, everywhere. (Big Brother is watching you?) He could hear what was going on in every corner of the place. And he could be to that corner in a matter of seconds if need be.

He was big, but he was "powerful big" and surprisingly swift. More than once Dick stormed out of the stand to rescue his monkeys from some sort of abuse. People inflicted cruel, unthinking pranks such as giving them lighted cigarettes with which they promptly burned themselves.

Such a scene! Dick's babies were hurt and they let him know. Jumping up and down, screaming frantically, they cried for help. The little screamers needn't have worried long, for Big Daddy was within earshot.

God help the perpetrators! They were given a verbally colorful invitation to leave. NOW! The monkey business created a lot of monkey business, but it was great for the kids (the big ones, too). It was a nice touch, a detail which brought joy to the little ones.

Eventually exasperation overcame monkey love and the monkeys were adopted out to the Woodland Park Zoo in Seattle. Dick visited them there.

Every bit of the work we did was based on a well thought out plan. All of us who worked for Dick found out quickly that we had better be there to work. We marched to his drum and we marched double time. Literally.

He said again and again, "Don't walk, RUN!" Plan ahead. When you see those people getting out of the car, you be ready. I don't want anyone to wait. Be sure you greet everyone who comes in. Be alert.

That translated into different tasks for different employees. For those who worked in the hamburger stand it meant, "Slap those hamburgers on the grill as soon as you see someone approaching the order window. I don't care if we have to throw away a few patties. I don't want customers standing in line." It meant having tomatoes and onions sliced, lots of them. It meant having fries ready to be dunked into the fryers, as well as fries all ready in the baskets. It meant that emptying the fryers into the servers was only part of the action. Fill the fryer baskets at the same time. It meant having all condiment containers, milkshake machines and cold drink dispensers filled to the brim.

Nothing irritated Dick more than an employee having to stop in the middle of serving customers to take care of a chore that could have been anticipated.

The "ever at the ready" mentality included the boys who were trained to fly out of the door of the hamburger stand to clear a table the instant a customer got up to leave. Hop to it, guys!

It was "Yes, sir", "Yes, ma'm", "Thank you", "Stop again". We could never let down. And we didn't want to. We wanted to please our big boss. We loved him and that was part of it, but it would be less than honest to deny the fact that we feared his wrath as well. He could be incredibly intimidating. It was a good place to work and he treated us well, but he was demanding. That was beyond question.

I suppose he found it difficult to keep calm. In addition to his volatile nature, Dick was under pressure to meet his enormous financial obligations. Attention to detail was his key to making the complex operation run in the black.

An example of his obsessive attention to small things is the story that George Valison, now a school administrator, tells. He remembers the day Dick walked into the hamburger stand, looked at a plate of cheese slices George had arranged and said, "Aren't we in business today?" That was all. Then Dick left. George was puzzled. The cheese slices had been arranged as Dick wanted them, in a spiral, one on top of the other so that they could be picked up easily and quickly. George surmised that the problem must be that the stack was too short.

He did what he thought needed to be done and added another two inches of cheese slices in their spiral pattern on the platter, hoping that that was what Dick wanted. It was. Shortly Dick returned, looked at the plate, said simply, "That's more like it", and left. Little things counted. We learned to look for them and then to do them.

Dick made it perfectly clear that there was always something to do. Customers were first, but any free time (and there wasn't much) was to be spent doing something constructive.

I worked in the stand. For me that meant making certain that cider cups, lots of them, were stacked at the ready next to the dispensers, that sacks (white, not brown) were in order of size under all three sides of the counter, and Aplets sample boxes were prepared and stored within easy reach. When we had a rush, there was no time for such housekeeping chores. All the attention had to be on service; speedy, friendly service, with an Aplet or Cotlet sample.

It was also my job to greet each customer who came into the stand. That meant I had to know which car had just pulled in, which visitor already had a sample, who had come in from the patio and who from the far end. Keeping track of the shifting, milling throng became second nature. Very few people were missed. I also kept track of which car people had gotten out of. Knowing license plates, I had information ready at hand — a conversation starter.

It was our habit to keep an eye on the highway, conscientiously keeping tabs on blinking left turn signals. This we did even when the stand and parking lot were full, for our continuous assessment of the big picture had an important bearing on what went on inside. When charter buses came along there was a swift reaction. "Charter!" Dick would shout over the intercom.

We followed a fixed routine. I would grab several boxes of samples and run to the parking lot. It was imperative that I be there when the door of the bus opened — a little sweetening at first step.

"Care for an Aplet or Cotlet sample?" What a great sales technique! Nice, too, in its own right. People liked the personal touch. I liked doing it. It was a detail that made a difference in how people felt about the place.

Simultaneously, Dick would fire up the popcorn machine and dispense help to the area of greatest need. It was a wonderfully effective system. And it was fun. People had such a good time that it was worth the effort. Dick was so funny. He knew that fresh popcorn smelled irresistibly good and that made people feel good. The resultant thirst effect also sold more cider. That rascal!

To keep the good feeling going, Dick added another touch. As the charters left, Dick sent them off with boxes of popcorn or peaches or cherries or something. It didn't matter. Word of mouth, you know. Showman!

During the night the stand was dusted and stocked. Baskets of fruit were made up in artistic arrangements, planned the night before. The final touch, the sawdust-covered floor was sprinkled down in the early morning hours. The aroma of fresh wet sawdust is in my mind even now. Each day was a fresh, clean start.

Most mornings Dick could be found sipping coffee, watering his petunias and making plans. He enjoyed that peaceful time. He must have been proud of what he saw.

Dick seemed to think of everything. Early on he made certain that his label was on as many things as possible: Tiny's Apple Syrup, Tiny's Apple Cider, Tiny's paper cups, Tiny's hats for the boys in the restaurant, Tiny's shirts with the boys' names on the pockets, Tiny's double cheeseburgers, Tiny's barbecued beef sandwiches, Tiny's tee shirts, and on and on. Name it. Claim it.

Tidy. He wanted the place tidy. I can't even fathom the number of pieces of paper I picked up, especially the little paper cups that the Aplet and Cotlet samples first came in. Dick could hone in on one of those from fifty feet. We walked the stand with our eyes always glancing to the ground. If there was a piece of paper in the parking lot, we were expected to double time it out there on a retrieval mission. It never failed. If we missed it, intentionally or otherwise, he saw it. Dang it!

He seemed to know about things that didn't seem to matter, but really did. He used to say, "Park your car out in front. That way it looks like we are busy, like we're open. It worked. Of course.

Most of the time that wasn't a problem we had to contend with. Usually there were plenty of cars. That presented another problem. Dick had his idea of how the vehicles should be parked. A place for cars. A place for trailers. A place for boats. A place for motor homes. Everything in its place.

He had a reason for concern. With the hundreds of cars that came and went there had to be a plan or the parking would be chaos. Gridlock. Parking, too, was a system that had been worked out in detail. On busy weekends Dad, Gary or Bill would be in the lot to direct traffic. One boat or trailer parked the wrong way could block the lot in minutes, as people had a tendency to line up with one another or do do their own thing. Creative parking was one more thing Dick didn't want to have to worry about. He had enough to do inside. Fortunately most days his planning avoided parking lot pandemonium.

With his country music, his source of comfort, twanging from numerous speakers, Dick occupied the nerve center, the command post. Details attended to, he was able to semi-relax, to be the Tiny his customers expected him to be.

A great deal of planning had gone into making those moments possible, when the real reason for all of these preparations came to fruition — the moments when the customer was Number 1.

Tiny accepted the challenge of change. Change brought us the landmark, "Tiny's". In the process, Tiny's earned a spot in Northwest lore. Change can be a good thing, especially when attended to in the minutest detail.

It took a lot of hard work to do the things that Dick expected. He expected quality. When a hamburger went out of there I better be darn good. I mean, he wanted it full. I've never seen a hamburger like we made at Tiny's. The meat that he got was the best meat and the buns were great big hamburger buns. And if someone wanted a tomato and somebody wanted an onion, we wanted them to be able to taste.

Everything would stop when the Forest Service called for lunches during fire season. They would want us to make six hundred lunches. And they had to be right: mayonnaise and mustard all the way to the edge. And you had to have ham and you had to have cheese. Two of those and a juice, a candy bar and a dessert, I think it was.

And we'd open up all of the sacks, count out six hundred. And somebody would run to the bakery and get all the bread and they'd bring in a pickup load of stuff. And then we made all of those sandwiches. Then Dean would put them in the truck and haul them to where the fires were. That was a real job and if you got a call, you were on call to come down and make sandwiches. They needed help, because they needed them in a hurry. It wasn't like in five or six hours. It was like you had an hour to make twelve-hundred sandwiches. It went on and on it seemed like, but we could really whip those suckers out.

—NOLA HENSLEY

15

TINY'S — ALWAYS IN SEASON

We place fine gems in a setting to showcase their beauty.
We build mansions on hilltops to feature their architecture.
We stage operas in grand halls to elaborate their drama.
When the beauty of one embellishes that of another,
the effect is stunning.
Tiny's originality coupled with
Mother Nature's seasonal grandeur created such a match.
In my mind I see a picture postcard.
I send that card to you.

Tiny's was blessed with an idyllic setting amid the orchards of the Cashmere Valley, with the snow-capped Cascades forming a distant backdrop. A visit there had rewards beyond the destination. There was the journey itself. The beauty of each season transformed all roads leading to Tiny's.

Spring — Orchards in Full Bloom

In spring, travelers were greeted by the fragrance and beauty of orchards in full bloom, forming a floral corridor to Tiny's from any direction. Along the roads, pink and white apple blossoms danced in a soft spring breeze, in delicate contrast to that of their showy cousins, the plum and the apricot. Cherry and pear trees competing for attention contributed their white flowers to the array.

Underfoot on the hills, secretly, mysteriously, minature bouquets of spring peek-poked through the earth. First appeared one, then another and another of the dainty native wildflowers clustered demurely amid winter-old foliage. Presently a whole field of them materialized where before had lain only the crinkle-cracked sunflower leaves from the past season.

Wild buttercups were the first sign of Nature's warmer side. Each plant with its single tulip-shaped bloom curled its bright head shyly. Among them grew fragrant bluebells. Shaded in blues and tinged in pink at the tip, they joined their yellow-flowered friends in a tribute to new life.

All the while, matted, monochromatic mulch was transforming itself into a spring-green carpet which would soon cover the steep slopes of the brown hills — background for clumps of yellow sunflowers waving convivially to blueish-purple lupin. All around one could see the freshness of another spring, the tender season come 'round again.

Meanwhile, the first big weekend of the year loomed large at Tiny's, with the anxiety that came from preparing that huge business for a new year and the annual celebration of the apples, the Washington State Apple Blossom Festival.

There was the spreading of new wood shavings, the hanging of the red and white striped awning on its three hundred-foot muscular steel frame, the unpacking and distribution of truckloads of new merchandise, the painting and cleaning of the hamburger stand, the planting of thousands of flowers, and all the labor that was necessary to fill the cavernous stand with products that had come to be expected of Tiny's. Jams, jellies, honey, cookies, gifts, jewelry, grab bags, souvenirs of all kinds, fruit, Aplets,

Cotlets, and cider all had to be displayed as only Tiny could do it. Massively, sumptuously, spectacularly.

When all was ready, the customer was greeted by the sweet-sour aroma of new sawdust underfoot, the clean smell of fresh paint, row on row of inviting products, a vast array of petunias promising an explosion of high summer color and, the bonus, Tiny all decked out in his bright, new print shirts.

Summer — The Valley's Full Richness

The early travelers helped celebrate spring in the valley and at Tiny's. The summer people would follow. They would have a different experience.

In summer, as fruit ripened and the orchards began yielding up their bounty, Tiny's became an outlet for all the richness the valley had to offer. Surrounded by the hills, now stark, dry and browning, Tiny's was at its circus-time best.

Rounding the corner from either east or west during the hot, sunburned days of peak season, the traveller was first startled, then delighted to stumble across a veritable oasis of taste and sight and sound. Flags waved invitingly from the long peppermint-striped roof and the petunia-lined roadside. Cars, boats, buses, and travel trailers jammed the parking lot indicating this was the place to be. Something was happening here. It must be something good. It was.

Finally, first-time visitors could actually see where the signs had led them. Return customers could again take part in the phenomenon of the most famous of roadside stands. The regulars, seasoned vacationers who follow the sun from Seattle to the summit of the Cascades through Tumwater Canyon to the shores of 55-mile-long, glacial-blue Lake Chelan, were among those who habitually dropped by en route. Kids, dogs, moms and dads with big plans for a big week stopped at Tiny's on the way. It was part of the tradition. State Park, Darnell's, Campbell's, and Pat and Mike's were among the destinations of these pale-faced Western Washington webfeet. Summer vacation at the lake was just an hour away.

"Have a great time. Stop on the way back."

"You bet. See you in a week."

Those days at Lake Chelan often produced a new look, as well as a "new feel". Many of the delicate-skinned vacationers now on their return sported peeling, mottled complexions ranging from hot pink to deep tan. A "Sea and Ski" fragrance emanated from the burn-tender, sting-hot sun worshipers as they tried to move about, often unsuccessfully, without touching clothes to skin. Tired, burned, and muscle sore from days of sunbathing and waterskiing, they were ready to return to the coolness of their natural habitat. Home beckoned until another summer season.

Meanwhile, a cold jug of cider, fresh from Tiny's might accompany them to the banks of the Tumwater where they rested briefly for a final toast to hot, dry days of Eastern Washington.

Over the years, many of the regulars became Tiny's friends. To have visited that place was to have become a part of the Tiny family. Customers were greeted personally and invited to browse, to make themselves at home. They were given samples, treated as VIP's and invited to stop again. Staff took a genuine joy in making the customer happy. Sales came as a result of the treatment, not in spite of it.

In the summer, Tiny's provided an experience that appealed to all the senses. Color surrounded the customer in the fruit displays, the products, the signs, and especially in the gardens of hot-pink petunias which seemed to be everywhere. The visual impact, added to the rhythmic twang of country music, pungent aroma of freshly dampened sawdust, and the fragrances of cider and fruit, created an irresistible blend of sight, sound and smell.

It looked good. It smelled good. It sounded good. It also tasted good. In essence, it was Tiny, his creation, the outer expression of his inner vision. Anyone who had been there needed no introduction to Dick "Tiny" Graves. They had met him through sharing his dream. Tiny's was an extension of his spirit.

It was nice to have met him at any time but, as thousands of vacationers over the years could testify, summertime was Tiny time.

Fall — Crisp, Amber and Gold

Fall, crisp and clear, ushered in the "amber season" when Nature's palette cast the landscape in a golden light. Somewhere a single, drying leaf fluttered to the ground unnoticed. A signal. The beginning. The end.

For many westsiders autumn meant the last trip east of the mountains before the inevitable snow in the passes. An apple run. Tumwater Canyon in its dressiest best enticed travelers to an annual show of outrageous color. Brilliant splotches of red and yellow foliage against the already magnificent beauty of the tumbling rapids and green pools of the Wenatchee River drew people into the path which led to Tiny's.

Driving out of that deep gorge of raucous beauty, one was propelled into the world of apple harvest in full swing. No longer was traffic dominated by travel trailer-boat combinations. Now it was the industry of apples. Trucks and trailers loaded with the fruits of the year's labors filled the roads with a bustling urgency to get their goods to market. Warehousemen waited expectantly to fill their storage rooms and the deft hands of packers and sorters were busy once again. Refrigerated railroad cars and 18-wheelers began the long haul, the distribution of fruit to world capitols.

After the celebration of harvest came the time when the verdant orchards shed their cover, when the growers rested briefly and planned for the next year. It was time for picking up props, putting away sprinkler pipe, pruning fruit trees and visiting with a neighbor while placing one's foot on the bumper of the pickup and absently toying with the drying leaves lying on the truck bed. Easing up. Winding down.

At Tiny's it was no different. He was anxious to close. But, first, there would be hunting season, that special time for the return of big boys at play, the interim when Dick could finally relax. Images come to mind: apples being cracked open by Tiny's big butcher knife, boxes and bags of red and yellow Delicious apples, fresh-brewed coffee, stocking caps and warm coats to fend off the chill of frosty fall mornings, droopy-headed petunias bowing out of the show, a fresh dusting of snow in the canyons, the Cascades obscured in their winter wrap, the hamburger stand closed and silent, a stillness settling in all around. The frantic pace of summer was over.

Winter — Rolling Up the Welcome Mat

As the fruit trees surrounding the valley on all sides fell dormant to nurture a future crop, so Tiny, the orchardists and the valley itself anticipated the winter nap, the rolling up of the welcome mat.

16

BIG MAN, BIG HEART

He was a tough man. He drove a hard bargain.
He demanded much. But he had another side.
He was unselfish — to a fault.
Those who knew him well were touched by his generosity.
In my view, it was the biggest thing about him.

Successful beyond measure, and grateful, Dick seemed determined to shower his new found bounty on family and friends. Anyone who was Dick's friend has a story to tell about how they were recipients of his generosity.

I was a beneficiary more than once. Dick doted on his little sister. His nickname for me was "Thithy". "Thithy," he would say, "I have a surprise for you." I was always amazed and never disappointed.

One day after school I went over to the stand to work and was surprised to find skirts and blouses hanging from the rafters. "Now, what's he doing, selling clothes?" I thought. It turned out he wasn't. He had gone to a fire sale at Miller's Department Store in Wenatchee. Ever the push-over for bright colors and lively prints, he had found some colorful clothes for me and couldn't pass up the bargain. He bought nearly the whole rack. Dick never did anything in a small way.

A dream come true! Six or seven circle skirts (the style at the time) and an equal number of blouses to match. It was lovely. A complete wardrobe all at once.

Dick's generosity didn't always take the form of money and gifts. When I was a freshman at Washington State University, I was so homesick I thought I would die. I wanted to go home. Dick understood. He persuaded Dick Odabashian of Aplets and Cotlets, a private pilot and plane owner, to fly to Pullman several times to fetch me and fly me home. Once Dick Graves flew over solo, having taken flying lessons himself. He just rented the plane and came to rescue me from homesickness. It was nice. It was also a thrill. While others waited for West Coast Airlines, I walked out to my private plane and was whisked into the sky over the Palouse.

"We can't have Thithy unhappy," Dick explained. I hate to admit it, but I was being a bit spoiled. Oh well, it was fun and nothing lasts forever.

By second semester, I had conquered homesickness and didn't need my big brother's flight service. He was, however, always there when I needed help or sympathy. It was pretty wonderful to have such a powerful and loving backup. They don't come much bigger.

No matter where I was, Dick always remembered me (others as well) on Christmas, Easter and birthdays. A corsage or plant would arrive from the florist. Francis Key, one of the owners of the Cashmere Floral, said that Dick spent much more on flowers for friends and relatives than he did on the thousands of petunias he had them grow for the stand.

Although there were many times when Dick spoiled

me with flowers or gifts, and those times were very special, making me feel like a little princess, my favorite story of his giving happened at the end of the summer before my senior year at WSU.

The day at the stand had been one of those Eastern Washington scorchers where one could actually see the heat waves shimmering on the pavement. We had been working in the heat many hours. Hot, tired and sticky, the only thing I could think of was a nice cool shower. My feet hurt and my back ached, typical of our physical condition after a busy ten-to-twelve hour day at Tiny's.

The charter buses, the tourists, the work with the fruit, the displays, the cleaning, the greeting of customers were enough, already!

We needed rest. At the point of tears from exhaustion, I was pleasantly surprised when Dick asked me if I would like to go for a ride to cool off and talk. Would I?

For one thing, it meant I was through for that day. For another, it meant I could sit down! It was always fun to ride in his big car. I have to be honest. I enjoyed the attention and luxury of being Tiny's little sister.

As he handed me a cold glass of cider and a sack of freshly popped popcorn, I settled into the passenger seat for what I knew would be a fast, cool ride, surrounded by the blare and beat of Dick's favorite country music. I loved it, too. Country music was part of my roots.

Hank Snow, Sonny James, The Statler Brothers, and Jim Reeves joined us for a relaxing, rhythmic, colorful, sunset ride to Leavenworth and westward through the steep walled Tumwater Canyon. As evening enveloped us, we passed through alternate waves of warm and cool air promising two things: the relief cool nights bring following torrid summer days and the distant promise of fall in the canyon with paint brush brilliance decorating its canyon walls.

As our mini-odyssey progressed, I had cooled off

84

considerably and hoped Dick would close the window. Fat chance! Dick was hardly ever cool. This was one of those rare times. We would do it his way.

One of the delights of an Eastern Washington summer evening is the vividness of the stars and the clear wide path of the Milky Way. Slouched down in the seat for warmth, my head resting on the back, I gazed at the sky as we rode and talked.

Conversation centered around the years of our working together at the stand. He told me how much I had done for him and how much he appreciated it. Suddenly the mood was filled with emotion. My eyes swam with tears and words were being choked by the lump in my throat.

I had worked at the stand since seventh grade. Soon I would be starting my senior year in college. The past summer had been an ending. We both sensed things would never again be quite the same. Some things don't need defining. This didn't.

As we came down from the town of Plain onto Highway 2, we had already begun another level of growth in our relationship. It was time for me to pursue my own dreams. I wanted to be a teacher.

We had left the stand about 7:30. It was now after 9. The parking lot would be empty except for a handful of people who chose to travel when it was cool. The hamburger stand would be closed and the night man would be busy sprinkling down the sawdust, cleaning or fixing the fruit displays for the next day. It would be a quick, "Goodbye, I'll see you tomorrow." At any rate, that was my expectation that evening.

A delightful surprise awaited me. As we pulled up in front of the stand, I was shocked to see the entire staff sitting on the patio. Across the front of the stand was a sign which read, "WE WILL MISS YOU." The light dawned. This whole ride thing was a ruse to get me away so they could prepare for my going away party.

Getting out of the car, I realized that tables had been moved out and in their place was a shiny gray and white 1955 Chevrolet. Quite a package. Pink and white ribbon about a foot wide, wrapped front, back, and sides, came together in a huge bow which covered the top of the car.

I had always had access to two or three cars which belonged to other family members, but had never had my own. I was speechless. A car of my own . . . probably the last summer to work at Tiny's . . . surrounded by people who loved me and wished me well . . . and behind it all, my big brother. Too much.

I must add here that before that little gray and white car made the trek to WSU, it received a new paint job. Would you believe — white with big red apples, the "Tiny" logo and "Sharon" by the handle on the door? Well, believe it. He loved me, but he also loved any opportunity to advertise.

Dick cautioned me never to drive the car over fifty miles per hour or the engine would blow up. Don't laugh. I believed him. I shake my head still at his powers of persuasion and my gullibility. Nevertheless, the car was a gift of love and I suppose, too, so was his admonition to obey the Tiny-imposed speed limit.

One of Dick's favorite ways of treating others was to take them to dinner at the Cottage Inn or the Windmill in Wenatchee. On one of those occasions he began reminiscing about his experiences in the service when he was stationed at the Presidio in San Francisco. As he talked he became more excited. "Would you and Gary like to go there?" he asked. I don't remember responding, but I do remember that the decision had already been made — just like that. We would go to San Francisco.

But, first, we would go home and tell Mom and Dad. They were in bed, so we had to wake them up. "Dad," Dick said, "Is it all right with you if I take Sharon and Gary to San Francisco?"

"Well, I don't see any reason why not. When are you planning to go?"

"Right now."

A few things in bags, pillows for catnaps, and spending money from Dick were all the preparations we needed. The big Cadillac flew through the night making its San Francisco run. We were thrilled by everything: the orange groves, the Golden Gate bridge, the Presidio, Market Street on New Year's Eve, the Cliff House and Fleischacker Zoo.

We returned, on the afternoon of a basketball game, with just enough time to change and make it to the rooter bus. As Gary and I boarded the bus, kids asked where we had been. "San Francisco," we said.

"Really?" they replied. "C'mon. Where have you been?"

"Really," we replied. "To San Francisco. Dick took us."

Then they believed. They knew him, too.

The California trip took place during Christmas break my senior year in high school. That was also the year that Dick supplied watermelon for the entire student body. At the end of the season at Tiny's, Dick had more watermelon than he could sell. He knew we were planning a bonfire pep rally just before the game, so he suggested we have a watermelon feed as well. Sounded like a good deal to us.

With kids, band, and bonfire at the ready, we began leading cheers. Onto the scene rolled the big white Tiny truck. More cheers. The big guy with the big heart quickly hefted himself up onto the bed of the truck where he cut only the hearts of the melon for us. Good fun. Thanks, Tiny.

I'm sure there are stories of his giving that I do not know. It was such a part of his nature that he did it constantly. It was not uncommon for him to fill the freezers and cupboards of friends who were " having a tough time". Turkeys, hams, roasts and canned vegetables were delivered in their absence. They would come home and, voila! Food for the winter.

I have heard stories of his sending airline tickets to

employees who were away at college and could not afford to come home for the holidays. That would never do. Kids should be with their families at such times.

It was also his pleasure to take the boys who worked for him to Mills Brothers in Wenatchee to buy clothes for their first year in college. "Pick out two or three pair of slacks, get the shirts you need, and a coat and shoes." He wouldn't take "no" for an answer. The joy was in the giving.

Dick took us all out for dinner one night and when we got through eating he left a hundred dollar bill on the table. And I told him, "Dick, you're crazy. I mean nobody deserves a hundred dollar tip." He was the last of the big spenders, to the point where it hurt him, you know he was having financial difficulties, spending money like it was being made out there in the back room. So I convinced him to take it back. I think he left a couple of twenties or something. But his heart was as big as his body.
—NOLA HENSLEY

People used to say, "Cashmere, that's where Tiny's was. I'd go on to say that I had one of my sons who worked for Tiny and what a great exprience it was. It really was. Ken was a kid who liked to have some enthusiasm and drive. So Dick was a natural. The kids who worked there had a great regard for Dick.

—RON DOANE

17

WELL SUITED TO THE OCCASION

Residents of Cashmere aren't long on formality.
Casual dress is normal.
Of all the residents of Cashmere,
Tiny may have been the most casual.

I can't come to your wedding, Sharon," he said. "I don't have a suit. All I have are my print shirts." Tiny's uniform was the floral print shirt, worn loose at the waist and draped over the torso of this mountain of a man.

Tiny told me it wouldn't look right for him to appear at a formal wedding, in a church, dressed in his "work" clothes. I told him I didn't care how he dressed, as long as he was there to see his little sister get married to her intended, Bill Hall of Filer, Idaho. Noone else would care, either, I added. He could come to my wedding any way he pleased, shirtless and barefoot if he wanted too, as long as he was there.

But Tiny was adamant. Maybe he could stand in the

back, he suggested, and then slip out before anybody saw him. I was crushed, but I knew that when Dick made up his mind there was nothing I could do to change it. I reconciled myself to his absence.

But I wasn't about to let him get away scot free. I had to involve him in my wedding in some way. Gary was going to be a groomsman, and I was determined that Dick was going to be in it, too. Finally, I asked him if he would hide our get-away car to prevent our trouble-making friends from covering it with graffiti and hitching up the usual battery of trailing cans. Yes, that would be OK. Good, now he was a part of the action.

Caught up in the minutiae of the pre-wedding flurry, I swallowed my disappointment and gave no more thought to suits or cars.

Typical of most weddings, mine was fraught with last moment glitches, not the least of which was a frustrating delay of the dress rehearsal at the Methodist Church in Wenatchee while we waited for Gary, wondering where on earth he might be. He finally appeared, somewhat chagrined but not nearly as much as we thought he ought to be. He had gone to the wrong church! Taking the oversight in stride, he grinned impishly, apologized charmingly, and topped off his performance with a Gary hug.

Forgiven.

Next morning I found myself the prime mover, getting everyone ready to go to the church: pressing slacks, finding matching socks, meticulously checking off items on my list, reminding others what to remember. Would we ever arrive on time in some semblance of order? I had doubts.

Dick dropped by to see how things were progressing, compounding the confusion with his teasing. He seemed in unusually good spirits. I thought he would be weepy — a family trait. Such a sentimental bunch!

Pictures were to be taken before the wedding, another imperative for punctuality. Miraculously, everyone involved showed up on time, possibly influenced by Gary's tardiness of the night before and the subsequent confusion.

The church was beautiful. Mine was a Christmas wedding, set amidst green trees illuminated by strings of miniature white lights. Francis, Anna and Noreen from Cashmere Floral had decorated the altar and pews with red and white flowers and satin bows, adding lots of extras and I was ecstatic. It was all so nice. My special day, my special friends, my wonderful family.

On emotional "overload", caught up in the excitement of picture taking, I was ill prepared for what happened next. Out of the corner of my eye, I became aware of someone familiar walking down the side aisle. Ambling along, blushing sheepishly was a smartly-suited giant, all dressed up for his sister's big day.

"Well . . . did you **really** think I would miss your wedding?"

Duped again. Tiny had had the suit tailored in San Francisco especially for the wedding.

As we left the reception, I shouldn't have been surprised (but was, having inherited my mother's innocence) to find our car was not as we had last seen it. Bill's pride and joy, a dark blue 1963 Chevrolet Impala, had been transformed by a professional, Pete Matson, Dick's sign painter. They had had **some** fun!

Two beatific, scantily-clothed seraphs, labeled "Sharon" and "Bill", had been painted on the expanse of the hood and captioned "We're No Angels". On the side panels were two sad-eyed basset hounds under which was noted, "It shouldn't happen to a dog!" On each side, from bumper to bumper was a two-foot-high inscription: "Just Married". Tiny had topped off his masterpiece with a quotation next to the gas cap cover reading, "Sharon's brothers, cider only, 100 spoof." Little wonder he'd been in such high spirits that morning. He'd been bursting with mischief.

Bill Hall, my brand new husband, didn't share our

enthusiasm. His dark suspicions that his prospective brother-in-law would not leave well enough alone had been confirmed. From even short acquaintance, Bill guessed Dick couldn't ignore such a delicious opportunity to paint another car.

Happily for the brother-in-law, and the car, it all came out in the wash next day.

(SCOTT and MARSHA GREEN, former employees at Tiny's)

MARSHA: I remember when we got married. Dick got real excited, but he wouldn't come to our wedding because he was afraid he'd cry.

SCOTT: He didn't want to cry in front of everybody.

MARSHA: But he was waiting outside the church when it was all over.

SCOTT: As soon as we came out the door he was there in the big car with the apple and everything. It was a Lincoln at the time. He had this envelope there and he waved me over and he said, "Here's just a little something to tide you over on your honeymoon." It was three-hundred dollars. Three-hundred dollars then was a lot of money.

MARSHA: But, like for graduation, he had such a big heart. He took every one of the boys I think down to Mills Brothers when they went off to college.

SCOTT: Basically, at the end of summer. He never told you. He just said, "Get in the car, we gotta go to Wenatchee." He always wanted someone to ride with him so you just figured it was your turn to ride. You'd wheel down to Wenatchee and he pulls up to Mills Brothers and he says, "Let's go in and do a little shopping." And this was before you were going to college and he was getting you ready for your college wardrobe, I guess.

He'd just take you in and say, "Well, what do you like?" You don't know how to react so you kind of just say, "I don't know." And he'd say, "Then how about this shirt? Does that look pretty nice?" And you'd say, "Well, yeah, okay." And so on. And that's how he did it. By the time you got out of there, you had four or five shirts, two or three pairs of slacks, a pair of shoes, a belt, and it probably totaled up to a couple hundred dollars worth of clothes.

92

18

DAD

The message is short, the effect long lasting.
He was a good dad.

Dad was just what a dad should be. There are some needs we never outgrow. Nurturing from our parents is one. No matter how far we travel, how successful or how mature we become, we return to our roots for strength and nourishment. Dad was the one we three turned to when troubled.

We loved that man. Superlatives are in order here, but the adjectives don't matter, at least not to anyone else. He's your dad, you just love him because he is. No explanations needed. To us our father had greatness. We had him on a pedestal. There's a lot of "Duke" in each of us. Dick and Gary, especially. We wanted to act, think, and grasp life like he did.

Our dad was a loveable, funny, wise man that others knew as Duke Graves. Tall and wiry, he presented a different physical presence than his oldest son. Inwardly Dad and Dick were much alike: humorous, sensitive, volatile men with a penchant for the unusual, sharing a common view of life. Both were hard working, creative, possibility thinkers. Gary turned out the same way. I believe Dick's and Gary's successes have come directly from the tenacity and pluck that was modeled by Dad. He could be soft and intuitive, tough and formidable. He was the dominant force in our lives.

To understand Tiny is to know his father and their relationship. As big as Dick got, literally and figuratively, he continued to look to Dad as his counselor when he had a problem. Wherever Dad was Dick sought him out. Usually Dad was in the orchard.

From the living room, we could see the road which wound its way up Yaxon Canyon toward the house, a perspective which allowed us to spot Dick's car the instant it sped into view. "Apples on wheels" flying our way with the speed of an Indianapolis contender was hard to miss.

The rate at which he cut corners indicated whether or not it was crisis time. If he skimmed telephone poles and tree limbs, Dick was on a "Dad Mission". He had a problem and he wanted Dad. NOW! His big car would hurtle into the driveway in a cloud of dust and a shower of pebbles. Unfolding his big frame up and out of the car, he would burst into the house demanding "Where's Dad?" Dick, having cornered the market on alarm, equated every problem with the end of the world. Dad had already been there. In his lifetime, he had pushed a few panic buttons and had learned how to cope. Dick drew on Dad's accumulation of experience and wisdom and drew comfort from his cool response to stressful situations.

If Dad wasn't in the house, Dick would stand out in the driveway and bellow, "Dad!"

"Yo!" would come the answer.

Homing in on the voice, Dick would set off through the orchard, not on foot, but in the big car, oblivious to the fact he was driving an expensive deluxe automobile. It had wheels. It could get him there faster. That was all that mattered. Up through the rows of apple trees he would bounce, spewing dust and leaves. He had the good sense to avoid sprinkler pipe, wooden props and low-hanging, loaded apple tree branches. Dick knew not to push Duke too far.

I surmise that as Dad watched or listened to Dick charge through the orchard, he must have been shaking his head at what he had wrought while wondering what the crisis of the day would be. Whatever it was, Dick needed an answer — yesterday. Typically, the problem had to do with acquiring fruit for the stand. Did Dad know the best place to get a load of cherries or 'cots or peaches, whatever was seasonal? What did he think of the price Dick had been quoted. Would Dad please call? Would he please go get them?

"They listen better to you, Dad."

Having been in the fruit business for years, Dad did know lots of folks and, yes, he would call or, yes or no, it was a good or poor price. Now would Dick please settle down? There was no sense in getting so excited. Dad worried about his son's hyper-kinetic personality. Dick had been nervous and excitable, even as a baby, he said, knowing instinctively that Dick's hypertension and abnormal weight were a deadly combination.

Dad was Dick's indispensable calming influence. The invitation to relax often was delivered more as an order and Dick meekly obeyed, until the next crisis. He was the little boy again when he was around his dad.

These times in the orchard away from the demands of the stand served as brief respites from stress. It was cool and peaceful there in the shade of the apple trees, listening to the rhythmic clucking of the sprinklers, and whether

Dad was sitting on the tractor, arms around the steering wheel, standing on the steps of a ladder balancing a bag of apples, or leaning up against the car side-by-side with his son, the scene was the same. Dad would take his handkerchief from his pocket, wipe the sweat and dirt from his forehead, light up a cigarette and listen. He could listen. Oh, how he could listen! He made it all better.

If Dick "Tiny" Graves was known by those in his immediate and extended family as the big man with the big heart and was extravagantly generous with his good fortune, he had a good role model. Dick was like our father, a thoughtful and generous man. If someone needed help, Dad was often the one who organized the effort to assist. We grew up with that example of concern for others. In my memory one such incident stands out. I call it "Buddy's Christmas".

It was Christmas Eve afternoon, that time when "If I'm not ready now, I never will be" becomes the standard exchange as people do their last, last minute shopping for whipping cream, scotch tape or the Almond Roca or Aplets for their neighbor who gave a gift and for whom you don't have one. It was time both hectic and mellow.

Dad came in, stood for a moment looking at the tree, silently for a moment or two, then said abruptly, "Come on, Sharon, get your coat. Dress warm. We're taking the Jeep.

"Why? Where are we going?"

"You'll see."

What ensued were the ingredients for my favorite Christmas story. It was a snowy, cold white Christmas afternoon. Dusk was falling. We climbed into the little red Jeep, closed the side curtains as tight as we could, and headed for town. It was then that Dad told me what he had in mind.

"You know, Sharon, I was just thinking about Buddy and his family." (Buddy had worked for us during apple harvest that year.) "He's out of work, you know. I bet

The Graves family visited "Grandma" about 1943. Back row, left to right, Dick Graves (later Tiny), and parents, Doris and Duke. Front row, Gary and the author.

Doris Graves, Tiny's mother, in 1970.

Duke Graves, Tiny's father, on his John Deere tractor, in the family orchard at Cashmere.

Tiny's younger brother, Gary, who is an equipment operator, owns a popular Cashmere tavern and maintains the family orchard.

Dick "Tiny" Graves attended Eastern Washington State College. This photo, taken about 1949, catches him in characteristic pose, feet planted, hands on hips.

they're having a hell of a Christmas. Let's see what we can do."

Parking the Jeep beside the brightly-lighted community tree in the middle of the main street of Cashmere, Dad and I proceeded to visit all of the stores. As he told the story to each of the merchants, I could feel the magic of Christmas Eve in a rush of excitement and pride. What Dad and the merchants were doing was part of what Christmas is all about. Giving.

The melodies of Christmas in the background, the tiny snowflakes that come when it's very cold, the wrapped gifts filling the Jeep . . . I began to feel like a minor character in an O. Henry or a Dickens short story. Dad was the main character; the plot and theme were unfolding. Life imitating art in a hometown. Like mine.

When the Jeep was loaded, we began our Christmas run. By this time darkness had settled in, it was snowing hard, and the Christmas lights on the big town tree were diffused by the crystal frosting now forming on its branches.

"Where does Buddy live now?"

"He's in a house up off the highway to Blewett Pass."

"How long will it take to get there?"

"About twenty-five minutes."

As we settled in for the ride, the heater began to warm up. The fan, on high, and the static, made it difficult to hear the Christmas carols on the radio. The whistling wind sneaked in around the door flaps, fighting for superiority over the warmer air inside. As we turned off the main highway the narrow headlights of the Jeep illuminated two faint tracks in Buddy's long driveway, tracks barely visible because of fresh snow and little travel.

Mother Nature presented a beautiful, but chilling picture. Naked apple trees lined the road, up to their armpits in triangular cones of snow. An occasional apple hung forlornly from a brittle branch, a white top hat circling its stem. Cold. We progressed slowly, little pitchforks of snow attacking the headlights.

"There it is," Dad murmured, as the Jeep slowly crunched to a crawl. A two-story frame house without a single light loomed in front of us. I was disappointed. All of this for nothing.

"Where are they?" I asked.

"I think they're there," Dad replied.

Getting out and closing the door curtain against the blowing snow, Dad and I made fresh footprints up to the back door.

"Hey! Buddy! It's Duke."

Silence.

Then, a light. Another. And another. The back porch light came on and Buddy appeared.

"Well, Duke. What the hell are you doin' here?"

"Oh, just brought a few things for the kids."

In the excitement that followed, wide-eyed little ones tumbled from their beds, ignoring the chill of the poorly-heated house. There was a tree but no presents under it. It was instantly transformed into a colorful circle of love from a community, from people who cared. Tomorrow there would be a Christmas feast on the table, toys in little hands, and warmth in the hearts of Duke's friends from apple harvest.

Nothing would do but that we sit down while Buddy and his wife fixed Dad a cup of coffee. In those somewhat uncomfortable moments, I was moved by the starkness, the chill. The children, wrapped in blankets, watched as Duke drank his coffee. We stayed only briefly. The celebration belonged to the family. We would go home to our own. As the red Jeep retreated the length of the long driveway, its own tracks almost erased by the sameness that snow brings, nothing much was said. For some things there are no words. The knowing speaks loudly enough.

The examples that Dad set made Dick a better man. Certainly part of the success of Tiny's can be attributed to the big man behind the scenes. I know Dick would say so willingly.

This was the man Dick looked up to. Indeed, we all did. This was the man who later was so painful to watch as alcoholism threatened first his health and then his life. The strong father of our youth was the antithesis of what drink made him in our adulthood. He had become someone we hadn't known in our growing up years. Here was a different man and a new problem. He suffered. We all did.

In mid-life Dad needed a drink to start his day and more to keep going. Insidiously, alcohol took control of his life while his behavior became that of the alcoholic, denying the problem to himself and others. He was no longer the witty, wise man. He was repetitive and boring, a sad spectacle. Old friends tried to help, but failed, then, understandably, drew away.

An enormous problem had been created, one only Dad could solve. The demons were his. We knew this; we had heard the rhetoric. Even so, we made sporadic, futile attempts to solve the problem for him.

Once, after I had married and moved to Seattle, Dick decided to confront Dad face-to-face, a "lay-all-the-cards-on-the-table" sort of thing. He had called and said, "Sharon, you have to come over and talk to Dad. His drinking is getting worse. We've got to do something. He's an embarassment to himself and people can't stand to be around him." Hesitantly, I agreed, wondering what we kids could possibly say to Dad that would make any difference. When I arrived home the next day, Dick was there waiting for me.

"Dad's out in the garage. Now, dammit, Sharon, we can't beat around the bush. Let's just go out there and tell him."

"Okay, but what?" I thought. We hadn't rehearsed this part.

It was a hot, dry day. Dust made little puff clouds

around our shoes as we walked the path to the garage. The hollyhocks leaned lightly against the building as though their ruffled blooms, hot and tired, needed support. Some things were still the same, the same this year as in years past. In the garage was change.

Dad was there, all right, standing at the work bench. He turned around, saw the two of us and instinctively knew our purpose. He said nothing. He didn't have to. The eyes said it all. The look, piercing in the squint-eyed dimness, so vivid still, was beyond pain. It was almost like terror, reflecting the soul of a man trapped between the vise of alcohol and the love of his children. The eyes pleaded, "Don't say it."

He turned back to the work bench without saying a word. Energy drained away. The heat in that enclosed place was oppressive, the mood taut with intensity. Moments passed. An eternity. The silence was thick. No one spoke. When we did speak, it was only words, small talk filling the space between us and our father. There in the garage with the smells of dirt and gas and oil mingling with the smell of fear, the fear of the truth, Dick and I were overcome by the power of the respect we had for our father. Even though it might not have been the right thing to do, we didn't, couldn't, cross the line which would have made him the child and us the parent. It would have been the ultimate disgrace.

I would like to be able to say here that the humiliation of the experience made a difference. It didn't. The problem continued. Even though the rational mind said, "No!", the physical addiction said, "Yes!" Alcoholism is a cruel, deadly disease, as intent on destroying its victim as any cancer. Like cancer, treatment is needed to stop it.

Dad continued on in his blurry, surrealistic state for years more before he reached deep for the courage and then the treatment to beat it. With the help of the Care unit at Riverton Hospital in Seattle, we all learned to deal with the problem of alcoholism. I wish we had known sooner.

As Dad's self-esteem, quick wit, and humor returned, so did happier times. The bad years fell away. The sad odyssey was finally over. Our dad was back. We enjoyed him for four years more before his death in October of 1984. Sharing our joy in this lucid interval was Nora Grant, a Wenatchee resident whom Dad had married after Mom's death.

It's too bad that Dick didn't live long enough to see Duke Graves conquer the hold that alcohol had on him. He would have been pleased, but not surprised. It would have been expected. We don't usually model our lives after someone who doesn't deserve it.

19

MOM

She was a nice lady, ever the optimist,
the softness of our lives.
I think of her often,
of the funny things she said and did without trying,
of her giving, of her in her pink and white gingham dress
hanging the clothes on the line, smaller to larger,
all in graduated sequence.

Our mother was the most gentle, unassuming person I have known, so when she told me of the time she went to battle, literally, for her oldest son, I listened to her with a a strange mixture of delight and disbelief.

Dick was about four and, according to Mother was minding his own business, happily making mud pies when the neighbor who was hanging up her weekly wash, challenged, "Don't you throw those mud pies at these sheets!" Well, Dick hadn't noticed the sparkling white targets, at least he hadn't noticed them until the neighbor captured his creative attention. The young chef stood up, proclaimed, "I will!", and hurled a fresh, sloppy pie at one of her white sheets. Splat! Now it wasn't so white.

Oh! Oh! Mother, who had been watching and listening was on the spot in seconds. "Listen," she said, "Dick wasn't even thinking of doing such a thing until you gave him the idea." The neighbor lady, who responded in an unkindly fashion, sparked Mother's ire even more. As Mom started through the gate, her adversary screamed, "Mind your own business and stay on your own property!" Too late. The protective mother instinct had already been aroused. The dogs of war had been unleashed.

What transpired was a scuffle in which the neighbor learned not to mess with Doris Graves or her offspring, for not only did the lady lose the argument and the encounter, she also lost a hunk of hair. A mother in her protective mode is a force to be reckoned with, even my sweet mother. It was a messy little business made even messier by the challenge from across the fence.

I was about eight years old when I first became aware of the close relationship that Mom and Dick shared. Dick was a student at Eastern Washington College of Education (EWCE, now EWU or Eastern Washington University). Perhaps I should clarify that: when he was a football player at EWSC. Mom was proud of him. She would say, "Don't you think Dick looks nice in his letterman's jacket?" In those days he was huge, but he was a trim huge and, yes, he did look nice in his letterman's jacket. Big guy. Big "W". Big man on campus.

Travel to and from Cheney was done by thumb. I can still see Dick setting out from the house on foot, Mom standing in the doorway watching him walk down the road until he was just a tiny maroon dot. She stood there looking long after he had disappeared. I don't know what she was thinking. I do know that I felt a terrrible ache in my throat as I watched my mother cry. It hurt. Mom was sad and I couldn't understand why. Only mothers can. Perhaps their sons, too. We couldn't see Dick's face.

Dick used to say Mom reminded him of Edith in The TV show, "All in the Family". One day he grinned at me and said, "Can't you just see Mom looking at her watch and saying, "Oh, look, it's five o'clock. Just think, it's five o'clock all over Cashmere." Of course that was an exaggeration, but Mom did have a beautiful, beguiling airiness.

Sweetness, naivete, gullibility, all were part of her special makeup.

They were also the qualities which Dick loved to pounce on. He teased Mom mercilessly just to get a reaction, knowing she was a great squealer when frightened. Mom often told of the time Dick took her for a ride up Needle Point, a hill behind our house when we lived on Flowery Divide.

Hiking this mountain on the dusty, pebble-strewn, ankle-turning path was risky business, so one can imagine what it must have been like for Mom the day she succumbed to Dick's pleading, "Let me take you for a ride up Needle Point in the Jeep. I promise I won't scare you. Come on, Mom. Please!" Mother gave in. Mother shouldn't have. Of course, he was going to scare her. Her sweet son couldn't resist such temptation. He was a very naughty boy.

The steep, well-worn path went straight up the side of the mountain, without switchbacks because it had to. It wasn't called Needle Point because it was a mesa. Mother didn't know that Dick was about to take her where no man had dared go before in a four-wheel drive vehicle. With a real "live", albeit frightened, passenger beside him, Dick rose to a peak of recklessness (no pun intended), cheerfully confident the mountain posed no problem.

Spewing rocks, Dick floor-boarded the Jeep and charged up the precipitous incline. Mom bounced around while holding on precariously to anything which seemed to be permanently attached, hoping she would be, too. Looking back, she could see rocks cascading down the tracks they had just made. Each time Mom caught her breath long enough to screech, "Dick!", her maladjusted son would laugh hysterically while assuring her that she would be fine. He didn't think the Jeep would tip over.

Poor Mom. She survived the ascent through dust and slipping shale only to have to face the terrifying prospect of the descent. She thought about walking down, but this was rattlesnake country and she knew they are nervous about company. Also, dried sunflower leaves vibrating in the breeze sometimes sound like rattlers. Scary. Pick your poison. What's the difference between being bitten by a rattler or being scared to death by a noise that resembles one? There really wasn't a choice. She would stay where she had already been frozen in fear.

Dick should have been spanked for gleefully bouncing that sweet lady in the pink and white gingham house dress around on the seat like a basketball. To his delight, as the Jeep careened down the mountain like a Brahma bull straining to throw its riders, Mom continued to squeal and Dick continued to laugh insanely. Not nice. Funny. But not nice. Bad boy.

It was just lettuce, lettuce, a few tomatoes, Best Foods mayonnaise, and salt and pepper. But you know what? That salad that Mom made was just about the best salad I have ever eaten. Mom's food was best. She made our favorites and nobody did it better.

If I had my choice of places to dine and a time machine at my command, I would go back to Mom's kitchen and have one of her Sunday dinners. Sometimes it was pot roast, sometimes fried chicken. No matter, it was always good. A part of the ritual was sitting around our chartreuse green and chrome table (we thought it was pretty) with the heavy matching chairs. While Mom busied herself making chicken gravy, we snitched little bites of chicken, getting our hands slapped in the process.

"If you keep that up, there won't be any left for dinner."

Her gravy was gourmet-tasty and smooth as cream. A little flour sprinkled into the chicken drippings and worked into the dark brown crispy bits soon took on the distinctive beige color typical of milk gravy. As the aroma filled the kitchen, appetites were notified that service time was near.

Not far away, waiting in a fluffy heap, were the mashed potatoes, the other half of a match made in heaven. Potatoes patted onto the plate and sculpted to form little craters for the gravy tempted a taste even before the other courses were passed. Add salad and chicken, a Mom and a Dad, two brothers, a cousin, and you had it. Everyone in his or her own chair completed the scene. I haven't had one of these dinners in years, but it is lovely to be able to go there in my mind. It brings everyone close, just like Sunday dinner.

Dick loved Mom's home cooked food. He would often ask, "Mom, if I buy a roast, will you fix it for me?" Of course she would. She loved to cook for anyone who appreciated it. She also knew it would offer her an opportunity to spoil her son while also affording her time to sit and talk with her busy big boy. "I'll fix you some sandwiches with the leftovers.

Then you will have some good food to eat after work tonight." It was customary for Mother to fix a lunch for anyone who had to travel a distance by car. "It's always nice to have something to eat in the car," she would say. Those of us who received the little road lunches usually ate them before we were fifty miles from home. There was something tempting about knowing what goodies awaited in the brown paper bag.

"Did she put in some of the turkey? I think I'll have some now."

"Me, too."

"What else did she put in? Okay, I'll have some of that,

too."

"Me, too."

I believe we live what is modeled for us. Mom and Dad were givers, not in the same way as their giant son, but givers just the same. The pattern was set. There is joy in doing for others. With Mom it was constant.

"Bundle up!"

"Put something over your ears!"

"What would you kids like for dinner tonight?"

"Do you have your lunch."

"I ironed those blouses for you today."

"I cleaned your room and changed the sheets. I hung them out to dry. They'll smell real sweet when you get into bed tonight."

Always there was the giving and the concern, the obvious kind that doesn't show. Momhood. It's many givings. The for-sure fact that you'll get a letter every day at mail call when you're at Camp Fire Camp. It's knowing that when the mail is picked up at the CUB (Cougar Union Building) at Washington State University there will be a letter from home with the unique return address: "Mom, 98115". It's knowing that inside will be an update on the doings in Cashmere:

"Dad will finish picking next week; Dick is getting ready to close; I bowled 135 the other night; I went to Dode's for lunch, she had a really good casserole with . . . oh, by the way, Penny got married." (This latter bit of new turned out to be vintage Doris. It was one piece with which I could not connect. I called home to find out. "Who the heck is Penny?" "Oh, you know, Penny on 'As the World Turns'".) I could count on being informed — about everything. She kept the news coming, the tie to home. Not everyone has that. I was lucky.

When Mom's guard was up for her kids, the entire genetic pool of the enemy was defective. "Well, I never liked them anyway. The whole family is like that." (At least that week, during the current kid crisis they were.) She gave support no matter what. Oh, we would get the little lessons, but we got to whine a little bit first. It's great isn't it? No one gives like a mother. No one defends like a mother . . . the bar association bar none. First line of defense, Mom.

With moms the giving doesn't show because it's so constant. We learn it because we live it. It gets in the pores.

All the winters of our lives, Mother was there for us, even that last winter when Dick died. Even when her heart was leaden with grief, she was a constant. I didn't see it then. I was too involved with my own grieving. For that I am sorry.

Dick's death meant that Mom experienced the loss of three sons in her lifetime. Can life offer up more than a human being can accept? I don't know. I do know that the days before Mom's heart attack were days filled with the suffering of the soul which permeates one's consciousness, filling every moment and allowing little escape. Must everyone bear his grief alone?

During the early months of 1972, Mother was under tremendous pressure. Her eldest son had finally succombed to the effects of work and worry and weight, the things she had worried about. She mourned for Dick, she worried about Dad and his drinking, and she struggled with her own blood pressure and angina problems. Her family which she loved more than anything was in disarray and she was dealing with endings and unknowns. For Mother, it all seemed too much.

When the heart attack came, it changed her status forever. It changed ours, too. We were the new care-givers. It was our turn. Her heart had stopped for too long, cutting off oxygen to the brain. For almost a month she lay in the hospital in a coma unable to escape from the hazy, distant other world of a damaged brain.

We rejoiced that when she did come back, she was no longer burdened with the suffering which had preceded her illness. She didn't seem to remember about Dick and she was always delighted to see Dad, who visited her daily. Even though she wasn't herself, she always sparked in recognition of family and those she had loved. Her sweet smile met our visits. I'm grateful. Without knowing it, she helped us through a very sad time. Everything was so strange and so awful. Ironically, we would have been lost kids without her.

Mostly, then, I remember Mom in her wheel chair by the front door of the Cashmere Nursing Home, expressionless until she saw one of us. And then, in the most poignant of gestures, extending her hands . . . reaching out to us. She was Mom to the very core of her being.

Somehow, it's recalling those hands that, more than anything else, brings her back. Pale, translucent veins raised, soft, worn . . . they were the hands of a thousand carings. I can almost feel them. Feel her.

It didn't matter that our conversations were limited. Her sweet spirit was in her still and we enjoyed her until the end. In the midst of the trauma of that year, Mother's presence continued to give us support. As always. She still does. She is our gentle side.

A mother's love is forever. The gift of life for all of life.

20

GARY

Like a roller coaster on a fast track,
swooping high and diving low,
a relationship has its ups and downs.
Gary and Dick rode the roller coaster a little too long.
It took them a while to get back on track.

Eggshell fragile, life experience tough, Gary is life head-on. Just as I cannot love one-half of an Almond Joy more than another, I cannot love one brother more than another. I love them both the same.

Dick and Gary were a lot alike. The outgoing nature, the "to hell with it, I'll do it my way" attitude, the belief in hard work, the stubborn determination, the outrageous humor, and the sensitivity were qualities they held in common. People who have known them both see similarities that reflect our Dad.

Gary was fourth born, the fourth boy. The first baby, Jackie, died shortly after birth and the third boy, Daryl

Duke, was hit by a car and killed when he was three years old. Gary eventually became the middle child, the one who was sandwiched between a successful, visible older brother whom Gary tried to please and an only girl, little sister, whom Gary felt a need to protect.

Gary was bright and sensitive, the child who tried hardest to do things right. He worried the most, which made Mother worry. Dick and I always teased Gary, calling him Mother's pet. Maybe he was. Perhaps he needed more nurturing. He was in the "sandwich spot". Mothers know these things.

I don't know why people are surprised that children from the same family can be so different from one another and have such different lives. It should be obvious that no two can have the same experiences. With each new child the dynamics change.

Sweet Gary, doing things right was important to him. One of my memories of this side of Gary goes back to early childhood. Mom kept a star chart on the kitchen wall with a list of chores and "good" things we were expected to do. Gold stars were, of course, the best. They denoted supreme behavior, red and blue stars marginal success and a white blank dismal failure. As one might expect, Gary the pleaser, was Mother's gold star kid. I was a red, white and blue star-spangled delight. Somehow I couldn't get into it.

Dick wasn't even on the chart! He was a big high school man, much too old and sophisticated for such nonsense. He was grown up and the owner of an orange and black polka-dotted Model-A Ford with a rumble seat. This strange color scheme was accented by its name, "The Lady Bug" and labeled as such on each door (I suppose a forerunner to apples and worms).

One of our greatest joys in those childhood days was to get a wild ride to school in the rumble seat of the Lady Bug. Never mind that we were forced to get out and walk while still a block from school. We grudgingly accepted the fact that we were the ultimate embarassment for our "cool" high school brother. Visualizing it now, I imagine a scene from the "Archie and Veronica" comic books. A polka dot car carrying two little kids in the rumble seat had to have been a little bizarre.

But I digress. Back to Gary and gold stars and eggs. Eggs? Yes, eggs.

For eating our eggs, we could get a gold star. I'd rather have eaten the gold star. Gary didn't like eggs, either. They made him sick if he thought about them very much. (Perhaps he knew where they came from.) He wanted them well done! Dick knew this. Dick liked to tease. I remember the morning Gary was having a particularly difficult time eating an egg that had not been cooked to his "well done" specifications. On to the scene came big brother.

"Gary, if you eat that egg you can ride to school in the rumble seat. Oooh, it's kind of runny, isn't it? Looks like snot. OK, hurry up!

"Let's go! What's the matter? Can't you eat your slimy egg?" Poor Gary! Waves of nausea ensued. I guess gold stars and rumble seats must have meant a lot because, through tears and gagging and merciless teasing, Gary accomplished the impossible. He swallowed the egg, earned another gold star and took his place in the rumble seat of the Lady Bug.

The classic Sensitive Gary Story is the one that was Mother's favorite. When he was five and I was three, Gary betrayed Dick and me forever. As Mother said (again and again), "He did the sweetest thing." This was not one of our favorite stories, but for Mother we good-naturedly suffered through each re-telling.

Anyway, Gary was asked to take his little red wagon and bring the wood from the wood pile and stack it by the back door. Well, sure he would. "Come on, Sharon. You can ride in the wagon." It was touching. It was the stuff gold stars are made of. I was the uphill load and the wood the downhill load. Mother loved it. I suppose I did too. At any rate, for this Gary was rewarded with another gold star and a handful of pennies. Then the gold star kid did the ultimate gold star thing. He divided his pennies with me! In so doing, he pushed the Mom button. What a kid!

Dick and I never gave Mom any satisfaction when she told the story, but I think we agreed. It was sweet. It was cute. And mothers don't forget things like that.

Those were probably the easiest years for our brother, Gary, because shortly after that when he was ready to begin first grade, a crucial time in any child's life, Mother was diagnosed as having tuberculosis. It was a very sad, confusing time. Mom had to go away to Spokane, to a tuberculosis sanitarium. She would be gone for a while, Dad said.

She was gone six months. I was too young to understand much. Dick was old enough to understand most. But Gary, the sensitive child, was old enough only to understand some, a baffling some. He worried. He cried. He imagined the worst . . . his mother might die.

Gary started school in Wenatchee that troublesome year, away from Mom, Dad, Dick, home and all things known. Gary and I stayed in Wenatchee with Grandma Graves and Aunt Aubrey. Even though Dad visited us every night after working in the warehouse, his presence wasn't enough. We were lonesome for our mother. Things weren't right. They especially weren't right for Gary, who had a difficult time of it in school, a bad start which would plague him throughout his school days.

From the beginning, Gary had trouble with reading, a tremendous handicap. As he got older, the reading problem caused added complications and Gary suffered inwardly while outwardly trying to compensate by becoming the funny, outrageous kid, the class clown, the good looking guy with the "apple" car. He learned how to cover his feelings and his thoughts.

We've all known such troubled learners, smart kids with school problems, often sitting in the seat next to us in school. Who's to blame? The home? The school? The circumstances? It's a complicated question with a complicated answer.

By the time Gary graduated from high school, little sister, the quintessential cheerleader and teeny bopper had passed him in school and gone on to Washington State University. Meanwhile, his older brother was making a name for himself in a dramatic way. Gary was a kid caught in the middle looking for an identity. He was in a bad place. Rough times were ahead for our sensitive brother.

Gary talked about his frustrating school experience once as a guest at the twenty-year reunion of my class. Standing up to speak on that night, he led off by saying, jokingly, that he had received invitations to three reunions and that he had gone to all three. We laughed, nervous laughter. He went on to tell us how he felt on the night of my graduation.

Something about the moment, the evening, the togetherness drew him out. Maybe it was community. Most of us had known one another since first grade. We had no secrets.

As he sat in the stands that night, Gary said, his mind was flooded with thoughts. He would be in school for another year. We wouldn't. He knew he couldn't quit. Dad wouldn't let him. Dad had always said that each of us could do what we wanted, but we would finish high school first. We had to get a diploma. With these thoughts crowding in, Gary described being overcome with emotion, bolting from the gymnasium, running across the football field, finally stopping in a huddled, shaking crouch beneath the Mission Creek Bridge. There, he told us, he cried. Then he screamed. There were few dry eyes at the reunion that night. We knew a kind of courage.

Gary did graduate the next year, giving cause for a

Graves family celebration! The clan gathered from Wenatchee, Yakima, and other points. We were proud of him. It hadn't been easy.

Love between brother and sister must be easier than love between brother and brother. Although we had our differences, Dick and I rarely argued, but my brothers often clashed as Gary grew into adulthood and Dick grew into his fame. In retrospect, it all seems so unnecessary, but becoming one's own person is one of life's perpetual struggles. It has to happen. The struggle was a complicated one for Gary.

Dick could be thoughtless and verbally abusive in his desire to get things done and done his way. He was that way with Gary once too often. In a heated outburst, he committed the unforgivable sin. He insulted Gary's intelligence, calling him a "stupid SOB" while berating him for a chore Gary had gone and done on his own. He compounded the insult by screaming that Gary was paid to do what he was told, not to think.

They had reached the breaking point. Dick had found Gary's Achilles heel and Gary left his brother and Tiny's on the spot.

It was inevitable these two strong willed men would eventually clash. Their "falling out" was a foregone conclusion. It would cause pain for both.

Dick knowing instantly he had done his brother a terrible injustice, was full of remorse. It was, after all, Gary who had been there from the beginning. It was Gary who had worked the 10- to 12-hour days without pay. It was Gary who could get twice as much done as anyone else. It was Gary who could be trusted. But more than that, he was family. He was a brother.

Dick regretted the demeaning, demanding outburst which had triggered Gary's departure, but this was one time "I'm sorry" wouldn't work. He didn't have the opportunity to say it, anyway, because Gary wasn't around. For two years he wasn't around. It took Gary time to heal and Dick time to swallow his pride. In the meantime, brother love was kept at arm's length by anger and separate lives.

If separation was hard, reconciliation was harder, for though they were sensitive men, they were also macho men. To such, no words come harder than "I'm sorry" or "I love you". Far easier to exchange expletives and mean just the opposite.

There is a happy ending. They did come together again. I don't know if they ever talked about it or, if they did, what was said. They never told me and I didn't ask. It's not important. What is important is that the love of brother for brother endured.

When Gary moved back to Cashmere, he gave a valuable help and support to his famous brother whose business had grown to much more than a two-man operation. When Gary came back, however, it was not as Tiny's younger brother. It was as his own person. It was as Gary Graves.

Gary has gone on to make a name for himself in Cashmere. He is married to Virginia Reeves Graves. He is the father of four girls, Gina, Ganelle, Gara and Gayla. He has been an equipment operator for more than twenty years. He maintains the Graves family orchard. He and Virginia own and manage a thriving tavern in Cashmere called Barney's.

He's successful, Gary style. He's a handsome, strutting cowboy (check out the hat) with even more of a flair for the unusual than his brother. Ask anywhere in Cashmere how to find Gary and people will know who and where. You can bet on that. He's an original. Another book.

He's the part of the Almond Joy with the nut in it.

21

THE TIMES, THEY ARE A-CHANGIN'

*This chapter speaks to my brother's angry,
sometimes irrational side.
It is the part of the narrative which is most difficult to write.
I would prefer not to.
I hope I can do justice to Dick's memory
and to those who felt his anger.
I do not want to diminish their right to truth as they see it.
To tell the truth as I see it, that is the best I can do.*

The Sixties. It was a decade of confusion and tension in which Americans were forced to confront a Pandora's Box of national problems. When our skeletons were let out of the closet, American innocence vanished forever. Television, radio and newspaper headlines inundated us with rebellion, violence and dissension. The events of the 'Sixties made the scandal of Elvis Presley's swiveling hips pale by comparison.

We were introduced to change with the "invasion" of four British boys who could write and sing and play in a way that spoke to millions. Boys yelled and shouted while girls screamed and fainted. The Beatles reintroduced us to rock and roll, made us think about their songs and gave us our new symbol of rebellion, long hair.

So far it hadn't been too strange. After all, the Beatles' new world performances were just a repeat of the public reaction to the likes of Frank and Elvis for whom boys and girls of earlier decades did the screaming and fainting.

But all too suddenly the sameness turned into a strangeness we couldn't understand. Asked to ingest too much all at once, we were on overload, feeling compelled to take a stand for or against and, no matter what position one took on the issues of the Sixties, the stance was fist-shaking rigid.

Witnesses to the violence of two Kennedy assassinations, fire-fed riots in Watts, civil rights marches and violence in the South, the assassination of Martin Luther King, the media event surrounding Timothy Leary, LSD, drugs, hippies, and Haight Ashbury compounded by the strife brought about in our country by Vietnam, know that that period in our history shook the foundations of our personal beliefs, as well as those of our nation.

Everywhere people reacted. Everywhere protest took form. Some marched. Some tuned out. Some fought. Across the land people struggled to protect what was their own, whether it was their beliefs or their property, or both.

Tiny was no different. A product of small town USA, images of patriotism impressed upon him by a World War II adolescence and army service during the Korean conflict, he was angered by what was happening to his country in general and his business in particular.

Dick's stance was double fisted. By God, no one was going to come in and take over what he had worked for. This was America. This was the place where a man could work for his dream, the land of law and order. Suddenly, in Dick's view it had become the land of long hairs, protestors, drug users, deserters, and all those folks who were so different from what had been the norm.

To Dick, the hippie movement embodied a flagrant

abuse of traditional values. It spawned the free hand-out, the sexual revolution, the emerging drug culture, the anti-war statement, and seeming disregard for the freedom that allowed such behavior in the first place. He was not able to accept the differences, the symbols of rebellion, the voices of dissent.

In addition to the turmoil on the national scene, a series of acts of vandalism at Tiny's, including destruction and defacement of property by people who looked like hippies, was becoming a real problem. Dick's experiences with some translated into a condemnation of all. In his eyes, it was unacceptable to look different. He took long hair, strange dress, dirt and foul language as a personal affront. People who fitted the description, all or in part, were asked to leave, sometimes told not even to get out of their cars.

"Just keep going. We don't want your kind here." He didn't seem able to look beyond the outward appearance of the inward convictions underlying the new and strange lifestyle. Result: polarization.

Dick fought back. He fought back hard. He made enemies. He became a symbol of what the dissenters were fighting. He was powerful, successful, and "establishment". Viewed as an Eastern Washington redneck, he became a target for theft, vandalism and contempt.

Dick's anger was typical of those who refused to have their view of the American dream tampered with. People were messing with his corner of the world. The turmoil of the nation at large had come home to shatter the valley's peaceful immunity. The people of Cashmere then felt the same bewilderment their big city cousins were feeling. The myth that a community could isolate itself physically and mentally from mainstream thought had exploded. It became clear that what affects one family member affects all family members. Americans were in this together whether they wanted in or not.

119

Just as the mood in the country changed, so did the mood at Tiny's. Just as Americans protested, so did Tiny. He protested in his volatile, impetuous way. It was his nature to react first, to think later.

Sometimes when troublemakers goaded him or vandalized his property he went after them. Charging from the stand, hurling himself into his car, and pursuing them at breakneck speed, he often intercepted them before they reached the exit to the parking lot.

Out of his car he would boil with a deceptive swiftness, generated by anger. To be trapped in a parking lot while being approached by this fierce, menacing giant must have been terrifying. His abusive tirade alone was an unforgettable experience for the objects of his legendary wrath.

When Dick was angry, his emotions churned up out of him and his strength was magnified by adrenalin. In calmer moments he maintained composure and settled for calling the sheriff or the state patrol, but that wasn't always the case. Sometimes he took the law into his own hands. He knew better. Stories abound of the ways Dick fought back. Some accounts were exaggerated, some not. Some of his protests were justified, some not.

That this big man was often filled with uncontrollable rage in those turbulent days is not exaggeration. That his strong arms once ripped a door off of a car is not exaggeration. That his big fists broke windshields is not exaggeration. That with one swipe of his rock-hard arm he knocked a man reeling over the hood of a car is not exaggeration. Dick Graves was an emotional man. In the heat of conflict, emotion often smothered reason.

To my knowledge, and relief, Dick never seriously hurt anyone, but the danger was ever-present. Because of his size and strength, his fists could be lethal weapons. I worried.

Dick had plenty of provocation. The new breed vandalized the fruit stand regularly. Some hippies and bikers came in looking for a fight.

Some trespassed in the orchards, making campfires under fruit trees and destroying them in the process. A simple hometown celebration such as the Apple Blossom Festival became a nightmare replete with drunken, drug-high people.

All of it happened. All of it became one of the great dilemmas of the time. It was more than most could deal with. Too much came too fast. Backed to the wall, people reacted defensively, like trapped animals. They came out fighting. Survival of the fittest.

Dick won the physical battle, but the conflict of the 'Sixties took a terrible toll on his health, his business and his positive view of the world. He became suspicious of the people he was committed to serve. Noone could predict the outcome, no matter what side of the political or philo-sophical fence one was on. Not a political animal, Dick was caught off guard in unfamiliar territory. Tiny was a human being out of sync.

As a result the mood at Tiny's was tense and defensive during that clash-clang time. The friendly "come as you are" attitude that had been Tiny's in the early years was replaced by suspicion and paranoia. "If you came in here looking for a fight, you've come to the right place" became the prevailing tone. Tiny put up a sign in a prominent place which read, "If you are a hippie or a hippie lover, you are not welcome here." That was joined by another which proclaimed, "America, Love it or Leave It". The words were inflammatory. They invited trouble.

I understood the problems and thus the point of view, but I disagreed with management's blanket condemnation and consequent rude treatment of anyone who looked like a hippie. I thought such assumptions were dangerous, that hatred bred hatred.

The prevailing atmosphere was unfair to customers,

most of whom were peace-loving, friendly travelers. Not understanding what had gone before, they were surprised, then angered, sometimes frightened. Irony. Tiny had created the same kind of suspicion and distrust to which he was objecting. His signs invited people to stop, but for the hippies, his behavior and that of his employees meant they would probably not stop again, unless it was to bring trouble. For them, and others, Tiny's had changed.

Dick and I talked about the problems but, because we disagreed, it created tension between us, a fragile truce. We agreed to disagree. We could accept our differences because we had shared history and life experiences, another irony. The answer was so obvious: knowing and understanding another fosters tolerance. It all made me sad. It still does.

On the outside the music played on, the petunias continued to flourish, and the signs still led people to Tiny's, but on the inside the view was different. It was a new view, a less naive view. The world could be scary and violent. Furthermore, it could happen right at Tiny's. Even giants could be toppled. Even legends could be vulnerable.

I believe if Dick had lived longer he would have resolved this conflict. He would have come full circle. Others have. People get a clearer view in retrospect, as time gives an opportunity for reflection, for putting things in perspective. Unfortunately, Dick Graves didn't have the luxury of time.

If this seems like an excuse, rather than an explanation, so be it. Tiny wasn't a legend to me. He was my brother.

22
MOMENTS

The years are long. The moments are short.
But we remember the moments.
Our last Thanksgiving together was such a moment.

For Mother, Thanksgiving 1971 turned into a hilarious, teary fiasco. It started out fine. The table was set with the best dishes and the fresh flower centerpiece was beautiful. I especially liked it. I had sent it. Candles were in place, extra chairs were around the table, people were sprawled around the living room complaining because the fire in the fireplace was too hot and shouting at the football game on television. Everything was normal.

Mother appeared and announced that dinner would be ready as soon as someone mashed the potatoes and Bill Hall carved the turkey. Good. We were hungry. As I mashed potatoes, Bill, the gourmet cook, took the turkey from the oven and began to slice pieces of the white meat. By this time Mother's Number One son had appeared to watch his brother-in-law carve.

Because of the whirr of the beaters and the whine of the electric carving knife, I was oblivious of the scene at the kitchen table. I looked up just as Bill said, "Sharon, we have a problem here. The turkey's not done." "Are you sure?" I queried.

"Well, for God's sake, Sharon," Dick interrupted, "the damn thing's bleeding all over the platter! God! We can't eat that!"

"Now what do we do?" Bill asked, calmly.

"Don't tell Mom," I blurted.

"Well, now, how in the hell can we not tell Mom," Dick thundered.

Good question. One to which we didn't have the answer. All we had was hysterics as we gazed at the bloody bird.

Mom, hearing the commotion, came into the kitchen. Dick, the ever-gentle child, bluntly reported, "Mom, this turkey is raw!"

"That can't be," she protested. "I put that turkey in at five o'clock this morning."

By now, Dad was on the scene. "But Doris, did you turn the oven on?"

Wrong thing to say. At least it was the wrong thing to say to Mom. She burst into tears. We burst into laughter. Dick was merciless. He announced it was OK, he liked it that way. He preferred red meat. More laughter, more tears.

"Well, what are we going to do?" Mother asked.

Never at a loss for an idea, Dick swung over to the refrigerator, opened the freezer and perused its contents.

"This will do," he said.

We stared in disbelief at his find. He had retrieved a package of frozen wieners.

"Here," he said. "We'll have wieners."

More raucus laughter. More Mom tears. Dick put his

124

arm around Mother and assured her that everything would be all right. He thought he liked wieners better anyway.

As we sat down to Thanksgiving dinner of mashed potatoes, sweet potatoes, cranberries, salad, rolls and frankfurters, Dick made a tremendous show of cutting and eating his meat dish. We continued to laugh, while Mom vacillated between tears and giggles.

Tomorrow she would get a new fuse for the oven. Tomorrow we would have turkey. It was OK. We had great fun. I'm grateful we did, for it was our last Thanksgiving together. Indeed, it was our last time together as a family.

The next months were to bring incredible heartache. Dick died in December. Mom had a heart attack in March. Tiny's burned in July and Mom died in October.

In retrospect, wieners weren't a problem. I'm glad we laughed together.

23

A LIFE LIVED

The end came without warning. It often does.
Even when it doesn't, the process is the same:
denial, anger, depression, acceptance.
It's never easy.
Life and death are hard.

I seek the solitude of the hospital chapel. I need sanctuary, a moment of communion, prayer and memories. I hear a stirring in the back of the chapel. I feel a hand on my shoulder.

"Sharon?"

"Yes, Dr. Connors?"

"Your brother is in critical condition. You know that, don't you?"

"Yes."

"It was an aneurysm. The hemorrhage was massive. We can't help him. Do you understand?"

"Yes."

Suddenly one's life comes to a standstill. Nothing has

meaning except the reality of life and death and the knowledge that any moment may be the last. It can end. We are mortal. The fierce desire to live is suddenly all important. Life is paramount.

Why didn't we feel this way yesterday? Why are our priorities so different today? Why are we now acutely aware of what is truly important in this life? Why do we see things with such clarity today?

Because yesterday someone we love wasn't lying motionless in a sterile hospital room hooked up to tubes and machines that rudely insult his humanity and erode our confidence. Yesterday we weren't in this "other world", this world of "don't touch", this world of fear which teeters on the brink of death.

We're frightened because we have a feeling this new strangeness could be the end of what is. We could lose this person we love. We don't want to accept it, not the tubes, not the sterile environment, not any of it.

Frustration. Anger. Take away the tubes and the smells and the sounds. Life is slowly draining from the big man who labors heavily for breath. Damn! It's not supposed to be like this. He's too big. He's too tough. He's too . . . "Tiny". He's not supposed to be vulnerable. Make him hear us. Make him come back. He's not supposed to die . . . he's not supposed to die.

The last few hours had been harrowing. The phone call had brought such numbing news, I found it difficult to collect my thoughts. My only clear thought was to get to Wenatchee as soon as possible.

The road was so familiar. How many times had I driven over Steven's Pass? Too many to remember, but I would remember this trip. It might be the last time I would see my oldest brother alive. It might be the trip that made all others different. because the destination would never again be the same.

Endings. They bring us to the core of who we are. They make us rise to meet fate. This would be a test.

Listening as my family told the story, I visualized the events of the evening. It had happened in Chelan. It had happened without warning. It had been an evening of basketball, Cashmere vs. Chelan. The hometown team was on the road and the hometown followed. As usual, their biggest fan was in the stands. Dick had been his excitable self doing his best to intimidate the referees while simultaneously encouraging his team. He had stormed out of the gymnasium, not well pleased with the scenario. He had calmed down, though, they said, before beginning his drive back to Cashmere.

Did Cashmere win or lose that night? I can't remember.

As he drove around the south end of the lake, the silent, latent killer which had been lurking in his brain suddenly struck, as an artery burst, bringing excruciating pain in Dick's final few seconds of knowing. Incredibly, in those minute flecks of time, Dick managed to maintain his grip on the steering wheel, slow his car, and guide it off the road. It was to be his last conscious decision. The big white "Tiny" car had responded to the giant hands for the last time. Silently he slumped to the side.

His passengers sat stunned with horror as passing motorists slowed, then stopped, ahead and behind, knowing something was terribly wrong. Their big friend had always been at the head of the line. He had always been in the passing lane, the fast lane. Tiny wasn't at the head of the line on this night. This could be serious.

Friends gathered around and helped move Tiny's great unconscious bulk into an ambulance. Then, like an honor guard in silent procession, they followed him to Wenatchee, to the junction. Here Tiny made a different turn. This time he wasn't going back to Cashmere. The others were. They would continue on. He might not.

While they waited for word of what was to be, Dick fought for his life. As it turned out, this was the big one. It was the battle he lost.

Later, when Dr. Connors talked to the family, he told us the autopsy had shown that Dick's heart was huge. It had filled a large part of his chest, he said. It was the biggest heart he had ever seen.

We didn't need a doctor to tell us that.

I was the first car there (when Tiny went off the road). He and Dean were in the car. They were just coming out of Chelan. I recognized the car and pulled over. And, of course, other cars were pulling over, too. He wasn't completely unconscious, but he couldn't respond.

We tried to get him out of the car and eventually did by the time somebody got there with the ambulance. It was a struggle. He was big and that steering wheel . . . he was just wedged in there. Getting him out was a chore. I'll never forget it.　　　　　*—RON DOANE*

He'd say, "I'm not going to last long . . . too heavy." I'd tell him to chop down a little. I thought he ate more than he had to, but that was just Tiny. He had a big tummy to fill and he was pretty well keyed up most of the time.　　　　　*—PETE MATSON*

He told me, "You know, I'm not going to live to a ripe old age. I'm not going to make it. But everything I do until then is going to be good."
And it was.　　　　　*—RON DOANE*

24

A DAY TO REFLECT

It was almost Christmas.
The sights and sounds of the season took on an unreal aura.
Funerals honor life. Births honor life.
Perhaps they are the same.
All of life is to be celebrated, endings and beginnings.
On that day we did both.
Time has dulled the sadness.

Outside, the sights and sounds of Christmas, the celebration of Christ's birth were all around, but for those of us on the inside it seemed another world.

It was a cold, overcast day, typical of Eastern Washington in the dead of winter. Even so, light shone through the stained glass windows onto the wall of flowers and the huge rose-covered coffin. From the loft in the back of the church, we watched as friends gathered to pay their respects to Richard Duane Graves. Uniformed, crease-perfect delegations from the Sheriff's Department and the Washington State Patrol filed in, silently, orderly, filling the first two pews. They had shared good times and bad with their stormy, generous friend. He had been their friend and they, his.

The people who packed the church reflected the years and experiences of Dick's life. Friends from all the years and walks of life attested to the diversity of his journey.

For the family this was a comfortable place. It was the Central Christian Church in Wenatchee, Grandma's church. When we were very small we had come there with her. There was also family history in this church. Our great grandfather had been a minister there; one of the stained glass windows which lighted the sanctuary bears the family name.

This was Dick's first church. It was also his last. It seemed a good place to begin making our peace with the fragmentation that death brings.

The service was filled with sadness, certainly, but it was also filled with joy. It couldn't have been any other way for, as the brief eulogies were shared, Dick's flamboyant, sweet, complex, sometimes obstreperous spirit seemed to touch us all. We cried. We laughed. We remembered. We wondered. What would it be like now, with this bigger-than-life man gone from our lives?

As we left the church, we felt a sense of joy at what this man had accomplished and what he had meant to all of us. His service had been simple, but dignified. A celebration of a life. It was good.

Tiny hadn't gone back to Cashmere on that other night, but today he was going home. He would be buried in the little cemetery in the heart of the valley where he would be surrounded always by the orchards, the hills and the changing seasons. The majestic Cascades forever would be giant sentinels as they had long been for the lives of the orchard people, past and present.

The caravan from Wenatchee to Cashmere stretched a long way, slowing as it rounded the corner and Tiny's came into view. The big stand stood ominously silent and empty as the big man passed it for the last time. One wondered. Was its life gone, too? Were the man and his dream one and the same?

As the procession wound through the quiet, snow-covered streets, the little town seemed to hold itself still. Giving Tiny his due. This man had been a part of Cashmere. It is the way of small towns. It was his way. They had shared life.

The people of Cashmere are gentle, hardy folk, unsophisticated in the ways of the world, but wise in the ways of life. They live close to the earth, experiencing daily the temporary nature of living things. They know death is a part of life. They would not be overly sentimental. They would say goodby, feel the loss, let it be, and move on. Life is to be lived as it comes. It is the way of the valley people.

At our destination, snow blanketed the landscape, concealing the nature of the place and its purpose. We were stunned by the scene and stood fascinated as giant white flakes began floating gently to the ground making the ending as peaceful as the beginning had been explosive. It was fitting. Everything about him had been a contradiction: outgoing, shy . . . a public figure, a private person . . . attracting attention, shunning it . . . flaring into rages, regretting the outcomes . . .

Always there was the flip side of the coin. Always the question: Who was this man of many moods? Who was this giant who so boldly emblazoned his name across the northwest landscape?

He was, I think, Everyman writ large, with all the hopes, dreams, fears and stuff of life that we all experience. The difference was that everything about him was bigger than life. Bigger expectations, bigger demands, bigger cars, bigger meals and bigger pants were the rule.

Nothing was ever really "tiny", not in the dreams and not in the reality. He became a living legend and remains a legend. He put Cashmere on the map and made his name synonymous with the Northwest.

Ironically, on that cold winter day, as a shocked silence hushed the valley and we said our goodbys, the legend didn't end, but continued to grow. Of course! He was that different. He was that unique. He was that man we knew as "Tiny", who brashly strutted through his 41 years with an unmatched flare and zest for life. He had achieved the kind of success that many only imagine. Four-hundred pounds of energy and determination and creativity had happened to us in the form of Dick "Tiny" Graves.

In all of the years of the legend-in-the-making, this was one of the few moments of introspection allowing final examination of a dream come true and then without warning ending. It was the moment of gentle goodby.

It was the end of the dream, the quiet farewell to our giant friend. We would miss him. We loved him.

Tiny was a fair shooter and an unforgettable gentleman. He left an indelible mark on all who knew him. —*BILL TARVER*

I thought the funeral was so nice. It was the way he would have wanted it. It was beautiful . . . the songs they selected . . . No, I'll never forget Dick. Never will. —*PETE MATSON*

25

FIRE

A spark of genius ends in flames.
Embers of remembering remain.

W e who had shared the excitement and wonder of the odyssey knew Tiny's Fruit Stand would last forever. We couldn't conceive its ceasing to exist. It had been part of our lives and always would be. At times it became our lives. That it did end was a painful nightmare, fate in its most heartless form as the last vestiges of Dick Graves' creation were stripped away.

A phone call shattering sleep is heart-pounding stuff. My immediate reaction was one of alarm. People rarely call in the middle of the night without some urgent need. These were my thoughts as I reached for the receiver, the third time in recent months I had been awakened in such an abrupt manner.

"Hello."

"Sharon, this is Virginia. I have bad news. The stand burned tonight."

"To the ground?"

"Yes."

"It's too much, Virginia."

"I know."

"I'll call you back tomorrow."

No emotion. No thoughts. I couldn't deal. Sleep was an escape.

Morning brought phone calls, headlines in the newspapers and lead stories on radio and TV. Still no emotion.

"Gary and Virginia, please understand . . . I won't be right over. Not yet."

First Dick. Then Mom. Now this. Pieces of the mosaic that had been my life were falling away. There followed a strange time as I experienced spasms of disbelief, denial, and non-thought, punctuated with frantic, panicky grief. In the back of my mind I accepted that these things happen to real people in the real world and when they do, we must deal with them. We deny it at first. We play "if only" as though that would make the little pieces of the mosaic fit tightly together again, but it doesn't work that way. It only prolongs the inevitable, facing life as it is, the new now. New pieces would form another mosaic, but they would never fit quite the same. The first pieces, roots, etch the most sharply.

It was time to go home.

I was prepared for the absence of the building, but I wasn't prepared for the emptiness inside of me. In place of the brilliance that had been my brother's creation was blackness, a void where his spirit had lived.

Dean Slechta, who had been Tiny's loyal partner for so many years and who had taken over after Tiny's death, felt the void, too. Many years later, he helped me recreate the scene as he had experienced it first hand.

Asleep in Tiny's old apartment in the rear of the building, Dean was awakened by a popping sound on his intercom, one of several which monitored what was going on in various sections of the three-hundred-foot wooden structure. He bolted from the apartment, clad only in shorts, and saw the hamburger stand's kitchen at the far end engulfed in flames.

His frantic efforts to call for help were thwarted by a dead phone line, already melted by the intense heat. He raced to his pickup, sped uptown and roused the fire department which responded immediately, but not in time to save the stand which was by then fully involved. The spread of the fire through the wood frame structure had been accelerated by the sawdust floors and tapestries hanging from the ceilings.

I visited the devasted ruins that day. Little remained. Tiny's metal desk. Broken cider jugs. The awning's twisted frame. Scorched water tank. Unidentifiable rubble.

The fire was another death, another grief. My tears finally came. Good. It would make the grieving easier. Emotion rushed from me. Good again. I didn't like the emptiness I was feeling. Letting go was a relief. It was time to move on. There was nothing here but the blackened remains.

Stepping out of what had been the gift shop, I was halted by the only color in all of this ashen mess — Tiny, himself! Hands on hips, bright floral shirt, silly grin on his face, smiling up from a stack of duplicate copies of his giant self in postcard form, he appeared to be having the last laugh.

Another surprise awaited. Nearby, lying haphazardly, surrounded by char, was one of his little blue and white signs, painted side up:

Tiny's, Cashmere, Wash. As it was in the beginning. The man and the sign of his time.

The irony, the black humor of it all engulfed me in an emotional wave. Laughing and crying at the same time, I thought, "Of course, you big goof. You always had a flair for the dramatic. What a showman!"

Picking up the thick stack of postcards, turning around and carefully stepping through the rubble, I looked up to see another reminder of Dick's special touch. There at the exit to the parking lot was the big sign, "Thanks, Folks!" My God, Dick! Did you plan this? The last laugh and the last word?

Well, if you did, I must say, "Good show, today and over the years." And I believe that most of the folks you thanked would join me in saying, "Thank YOU, big man, for sharing your dreams and your hospitality. We had a good time at the circus."

The show has closed, the tent has folded and the ringmaster has gone. Center ring will never again be the same.

EPILOG

After the fire, Dean took some time to rethink his future. Finally, he rebuilt Tiny's.

Dean called it "Tiny's of Cashmere", creating a more modest copy of the giant original. He kept the dream alive for nine years more until November 1981. During that period he married Gerri Webb, who helped him run the stand. The stand and roadside property were sold to make room for a supermarket. Tiny's of Cashmere eventually found a home in Leavenworth a few miles west.

Dean was with Tiny almost from the start, staying on to become a partner in the burgeoning business. Except for a brief service hiatus, he saw it all firsthand, putting in years of long hours and hard work for his volatile friend and partner — his patience and loyalty contributing a needed balance to the business.

I don't see Dean much anymore. But recently we spent an enjoyable afternoon reminiscing. We remembered the wild ride we had shared on Tiny's runaway train, touching on the highlights, from an encounter with a hippie, a peach pincher or just one of those hellishly hot summer days,

We agreed on one thing. It was hard to believe it had all happened.